brilliant

how to manage your time

PEARSON

At Pearson, we believe in learning – all kinds of learning for all kinds of people. Whether it's at home, in the classroom or in the workplace, learning is the key to improving our life chances.

That's why we're working with leading authors to bring you the latest thinking and best practices, so you can get better at the things that are important to you. You can learn on the page or on the move, and with content that's always crafted to help you understand quickly and apply what you've learned.

If you want to upgrade your personal skills or accelerate your career, become a more effective leader or more powerful communicator, discover new opportunities or simply find more inspiration, we can help you make progress in your work and life.

Pearson is the world's leading learning company. Our portfolio includes the Financial Times and our education business, Pearson International.

Every day our work helps learning flourish, and wherever learning flourishes, so do people.

To learn more, please visit us at **www.pearson.com/uk**

how to manage your time

Mike Clayton

PEARSON

Harlow, England • London • New York • Boston • San Francisco • Toronto • Sydney • Auckland • Singapore • Hong Kong
Tokyo • Seoul • Taipei • New Delhi • Cape Town • São Paulo • Mexico City • Madrid • Amsterdam • Munich • Paris • Milan

PEARSON EDUCATION LIMITED
Edinburgh Gate
Harlow CM20 2JE
United Kingdom
Tel: +44 (0)1279 623623
Web: www.pearson.com/uk

First published in Great Britain as *Brilliant Time Management* in 2011 (print and electronic)
Rejacketed edition published 2015 (print and electronic)

Pearson Education is not responsible for the content of third-party internet sites.

ISBN: 978-1-292-08326-1 (print)
       978-1-292-08400-8 (PDF)
       978-1-292-08406-0 (eText)
       978-1-292-08399-5 (ePub)

British Library Cataloguing-in-Publication Data
A catalogue record for the print edition is available from the British Library

Library of Congress Cataloging-in-Publication Data
A catalog record for the print edition is available from the Library of Congress

10 9 8 7 6 5 4 3 2 1
18 17 16 15 14

Series cover design by David Carroll & Co

Print edition typeset in 10/14 pt Plantin MT Pro by 71
Printed in Great Britain by Henry Ling Ltd, at the Dorset Press, Dorchester, Dorset

NOTE THAT ANY PAGE CROSS REFERENCES REFER TO THE PRINT EDITION

To Felicity, who gave me the time to write this book; and to Sophia, who brings new meanings to time.

Contents

About the author

Mike Clayton started working life in the academic world and has since been a consultant and project manager, a trainer and executive coach, and a facilitator and speaker. Throughout this time, he has built a reputation as a master of getting things done. Over the last ten years, he has studied the techniques that successful people use to meet deadlines and achieve huge amounts. He has brought his expertise as a professional project manager to bear and combined it with his understanding of psychology to develop a large toolbox of time-management resources that really work. Mike has trained and spoken extensively on the subjects of project management and time management, helping people to get more done, from the largest project to the smallest job.

Mike has a science PhD from the University of Manchester and is an NLP Master Practitioner. As a volunteer, he has been a Chair of Governors and a trustee of two charities.

Introduction

When I was a student, I had a beard. I figured that for each day I did not shave, I was saving myself at least five minutes, so that over the course of a week, I would save half an hour or more. In a year, I could easily save a whole day – 24 hours. I loved student life and, from my pre-university stint in a research lab to accepting a 'proper' job, I spent seven glorious years studying, researching and having fun. And, as a bonus, by not shaving every day for those seven years, I had saved a whole week.

So when sudden and sad events forcibly delayed the start of this book, I consoled myself with knowing that I could still meet the publisher's deadline, because I had seven days of time saved from my university life.

You cannot save time

But where were those seven days? Of course, this story highlights the truth that we cannot 'save' time: it isn't like any other resource. All we can do is use the time we have wisely.

This book cannot save you time. What it will do is give you the tools to use the time you have to do more of the things you want to do, to get the things you have to do finished – on time, to get your work done more efficiently, to achieve what you consider to be success.

How much you want to get done is your choice. If something matters to you, I will show you how to prioritise it, how to plan it, how to focus on it, how to get people to help you with it, and how to get it done.

So, whether your time troubles are that you have too much to do, too little time, too many interruptions, or you keep putting off what you know you have to do, this book has the answers you need.

As a teenager and throughout my adult life, I have built a reputation for getting loads done. It has not always been easy, as I have found myself working on tough work assignments with pressing deadlines and a host of other responsibilities to discharge. I have found ways to deal with this pressure and deliver on time which work for me. Over the last ten years I have looked for more approaches, so that I can help other people to take control of their time and their task lists too. The ideas in this book work. They are in a logical sequence and each chapter will help you to build your resources steadily and see how some ideas contribute to others.

The chapters and their themes

The eleven chapters of this book each have a theme, and the following list summarises them, to help a casual 'dip-in-and-out' reader.

Part 1: The basics of how to manage your time

Chapter 1: What is your attitude to time?

The theme of this chapter is 'attitude'. This section will introduce the three principal attitudes of past, present and future orientation, and you will learn how to create a sensible balance.

Chapter 2: Understand how you use your time

The theme of this chapter is 'awareness'. As you become aware of where your time goes, you can start to identify the time-management problems you need to solve, and so recognise the solutions in this book that will help you.

Chapter 3: Six fundamentals of how to manage your time

The theme of this chapter is 'fundamentals'. Here you will see six basic disciplines to practise, which will bring your response to getting things done and using your time effectively under your control.

Chapter 4: Know what you are doing things for

The theme of this chapter is 'goals'. Effective time management must sit in the context of knowing what you want, and this chapter will introduce powerful tools to show you how to identify your goals over short-, medium- and long-term horizons.

Part 2: Work effectively and avoid the pitfalls that steal your time

Chapter 5: How to do things effectively

The theme of this chapter is 'effectiveness'. There are huge benefits when you focus precisely on one task, while there are also advantages to being able to tackle many things at once. We will explore the multi-tasking fallacy, the traps of both extremes of behaviour, and how to deal with the typical consequence: stress. We will also look at how you can be more effective in two crucial contexts where people commonly spend a lot of un-productive time: reading and meetings.

Chapter 6: Focus on priorities to take control of your time

The theme of this chapter is 'priorities'. Understand the distinction between what is important and what is merely urgent. Avoiding the pressures to be busy-busy all the time or waiting until something is too late will allow you to focus on your priorities. This chapter will deal with time stealers, the drive to 'hurry up' and ways to conquer procrastination.

Chapter 7: When to keep going and when to let go

The theme of this chapter is 'focus'. It's not just about getting things done; it's about sticking at the right things and dropping things that don't matter. This chapter is about making choices and letting go of the projects and ideas that do not fit into your future. You will also learn how the balance between work that is too challenging and work that is too easy can lead to peak productivity.

Chapter 8: Who are you doing things for?

The theme of this chapter is saying 'no'. Why do we do things for other people when we know they don't really appreciate it? Some of us do it because we see burden as our role in life, while others just want to please people. Prioritise the calls on your time and make effective decisions so that you are doing things for you. Learn a new way to think about a vital skill: the ability to say 'NO'.

Part 3: Ultimate success in getting things done

Chapter 9: Using other people to get things done

The theme of this chapter is 'delegation'. Effective delegation is a classic part of your time-management repertoire, so this chapter looks at it carefully, to understand why so many of us find it difficult and to give you a process and tools to support you in doing it well.

Chapter 10: The OATS principle: the ultimate process for how to manage your time

The theme of this chapter is getting your 'OATS'. It will introduce you to a simple, powerful process, the OATS principle, for planning your time. This will be supported by tips and techniques to use the OATS principle effectively, and time management tools based on the OATS principle.

Chapter 11: The three things exceptional time managers do
The theme of this chapter is 'planning'. This chapter will give a final review of the aspects of how to manage your time, drawing everything together with ideas about how to plan ahead, protect what you have and create time to think.

So what will you get from this book?

Some people reading this book would say that they want more time for the 'choose to' things in their life, rather than the 'have to' things. I call you the 'stuck at must' readers.

Some people reading this book would say that they want to get more of their jobs done – whether work, social, family or anything else. I call you the 'stuck at some' readers.

Some people reading this book would say that they don't seem to be moving forward with their lives, their work, or their dreams. I call you the 'stuck at now' readers.

Some people reading this book would say that they seem to be forever frustrated in getting what they want done, because other people's priorities keep intruding. I call you the 'stuck with stuff' readers.

Read on if you want to:

1. Start to see how some of your 'have to' activities can enhance your life and so become 'choose to' activities. You will particularly like Chapter 4. This will especially appeal to 'stuck at must' and 'stuck at now' readers.
2. Do more with the time you have available. You will particularly like Chapters 3, 5, 10 and 11. These will especially appeal to the 'stuck at some' and 'stuck at now' readers.
3. Commit to fewer of the 'have to' things in your life. You will particularly like Chapters 6 and 8. These will especially appeal to the 'stuck at must' and 'stuck with stuff' readers.

4. Create more time opportunities to do the 'choose to' things you want to focus on. You will particularly like Chapter 7. This will especially appeal to the 'stuck at must' and 'stuck at now' readers.

5. Get somebody else to do some of your 'have to' things for you. You will particularly like Chapter 9. This will especially appeal to the 'stuck at must' and 'stuck at some' readers.

6. Learn a fundamental process for getting things done and planning your time. You will particularly like Chapter 10. This will especially appeal to the 'stuck at some' and 'stuck at now' readers.

What all of these strategies have in common is the need to take a positive and proactive approach to using your time. You cannot have more time; all you can do is use what you do have well.

Author acknowledgements

There are too many diverse influences on my life to identify any individuals to thank for the time-management knowledge and skills I have acquired along the way. However, I do want to mention the phenomenal group of people I worked with during my years in consultancy, working in the firm that is now called Deloitte. Ultimately, what all of you taught me is just how much it is possible for determined and able people to do. You gave reality to the old saying: 'if you want something done, ask a busy person.'

I also want to thank my editor, Samantha Jackson, for figuring out why my original draft felt wrong.

PART 1

The basics of how to manage your time

P art 1 of *How to Manage Your Time* sets the groundwork for your time-management skills by setting out the four basics for success:

First   You need to understand your own attitudes to time. There are no right or wrong attitudes, but some attitudes will help you to manage your time to get more done in the time you have. Chapter 1 will show you what the different attitudes are, and give you the tools you need to help shift the balance to the attitudes that will help you to manage your time.

Second   You also need to understand how you use your time, so Chapter 2 gives you the tools that you need to monitor where your time goes and to also put a value on your time. At the end of the chapter, you will read how common patterns can be addressed by the tools in Parts 2 and 3 of *How to Manage Your Time*.

Third   The third pre-requisite for success is to get the fundamentals in place, so Chapter 3 will tell you what these are.

Fourth   Before you can manage your time effectively, you must also know what you are doing things for. Chapter 4 will give you a range of tools to set goals that will give purpose to your time management.

CHAPTER 1

What is your attitude to time?

T his chapter is about your attitude to time, and why that attitude dictates how productively you use time. We will see that there are three fundamental time orientations, and how each can have advantages and disadvantages for us. Before you can manage your time effectively, you must bring balance to these different attitudes. By the end of this chapter, you will understand what your attitude to time is and what your priorities are to help balance it and improve your time management.

The three fundamental orientations are past, present and future. We will examine these one at a time, and then see where a good balance lies.

Past orientation

If you have a predominantly past orientation you will spend a lot of your time dwelling on the past, so that it can have a huge impact on your present and therefore also on your future. How you remember and interpret past events affects not just your attitude, but your current and future choices. While there are advantages and disadvantages to a past orientation, what is central to your wellbeing is whether you have a predominantly positive or negative attitude to your past.

Positive past attitudes

A positive attitude to your past is characterised by a focus on the good things that have happened to you and events that have brought you pleasure and satisfaction. People with a positive attitude to their past tend to think less about adverse events and, when they do think about them, see their positive aspects – how well they coped, what they learned and the good things that came out of troubled times. For these reasons, if you have a positive attitude to your past, you probably enjoy reflecting back and like to keep and look at old photos and videos, you probably enjoy the nostalgia of re-reading favourite books or listening to old music, and you certainly cherish being with old friends.

Negative past attitudes

A negative attitude to your past means that the past dominates your present in a destructive way. You reflect on painful experiences to the exclusion of the good things that have happened to you, which can leave you bitter, frustrated, even angry with the world. You tend to stay busy and can get a lot done, but this is merely a way of shutting out painful memories, so that productivity is equally likely to be in fruitless tasks as it is to be directed towards useful ends. Indeed, it is unlikely that people with a negative attitude to their past will look forward to the future; they are more likely to anticipate that it will be just as bad as their perception of the past.

How a past orientation can get things done

Although a negative attitude to the past can trigger manic activity to exclude memories, this is not helpful. A positive past orientation, however, can help as it gives you a clear and meaningful sense of who you are and what your place is in your personal history. This leaves you feeling confident about your future. We tend to allow our perception of the past to drive our decisions about the future and, while there is a risk of over-optimism, if

you are positive about your past you are likely to make coura-
geous, confident choices about your future.

On the other hand, the danger of being too past-oriented is that
it can frustrate your ability to get things done and to make good
use of the time you have. With a negative attitude, there can be a
sense of futility and a lack of desire to seek out pleasures that you
could see as ultimately doomed to failure. Positive attitudes to
your past can also hold you back, if the sense of nostalgia leaves
you feeling too comfortable living on your memories.

Present orientation

Your average sloth can cover nearly five metres in a minute when
pushed to escape from one of South America's few predators.
For them, this is speed indeed, and it uses up a lot of their precious energy. The poor creature is the only one to share a name
with one of the seven deadly sins, but in truth it is constrained
by its environment: the leaves it eats can take over a month to
digest. Nonetheless, sloths have come to symbolise a 'don't care'
attitude to time.

Mayflies, on the other hand, can live for up to a few days, with
some species having only a matter of minutes to live their lives,
find a mate and attend to the next generation before their
allotted time is over. Imagine how knowing you had only one day
to live would affect your perception of time – especially if there
were things you really wanted to achieve. Mayflies symbolise a
'live for the moment' attitude to time.

These two extreme examples of a present orientation
towards time.

Negative present attitudes

The sloth represents an apathetic sense that nothing is worth
bothering with; people with this attitude are neither enthusiastic

nor conscientious about anything and they are prone to self-destructive behaviours that follow from a sense of pointlessness.

Positive present attitudes

The mayfly represents the opposite end of the spectrum; an attitude where life is entirely about the present moment. Mayflies tend to be fun-seeking, adventurous people who are spontaneous to the point of disrupting and unsettling those around them. They too can indulge in self-destructive behaviour, but their motivation is to get a buzz from the experience of high-risk or addictive activities. Don't expect a mayfly to keep a diary or even wear a watch!

How a present orientation can get things done

The sloth attitude has one big advantage: if you are not rushing around to get things done, then maybe you can slow down to enjoy the moment. Likewise, the mayfly attitude also has a big benefit to you: if you are concerned to get lots done, then, properly directed, it can be a source of huge energy that will allow you to achieve great things. What is important, however, is that the great things you achieve are also worthwhile.

Future orientation

If you have a future orientation, the future is the driving force to your thinking and decision making. Consequently, you are likely to plan ahead to achieve what is important to you in a longer time frame and work diligently to achieve it. This can apply to your own personal future and also to that of your family, your business, or any other organisations you are involved in. This makes people with a future-oriented attitude to time highly conscientious and reliable; you can expect them to arrive on time and stick with a job until it gets done. However, they can also be prone to anxiety and stress, and feel a need to make sacrifices now to work towards the future.

How a future orientation can get things done

Clearly a future orientation is well-suited to setting goals, active time planning and diligent work to achieve your goals. If you are future oriented, this makes you an enthusiastic problem-solver with a determination to succeed, which can over-ride your current needs. On the face of it, this is the orientation to have, if you want to get things done. There are, however, problems.

How a future orientation can get in the way

In not paying attention to your current needs you can become obsessed with achievement for its own sake; you take on too much, and never find the fulfilment you seek because you constantly sacrifice your present enjoyment for perceived future gains.

Another important trap that people with a future orientation fall into is to try to resolve problems that are outside of their control. One immediate way for you to review your workload is to make a clear distinction between the things that are within your control and the things you cannot control.

Too often we find our workload dominated by outcomes we cannot control. This causes us to dissipate a lot of our energy into trying to achieve something without all of the resources or authority that we need. The next chapter will help you to make this distinction even clearer, because the real challenge is in how to deal with outcomes that are partly in our control.

What's your attitude?

So what did you discover as you read through the three different attitudes to time? It's likely that you saw yourself in each of the categories, to lesser or greater degrees, and that you were able to identify whether you have more of a positive or negative attitude within each orientation. If you discovered that, on the whole, you are not happy with the attitudes you have towards time, don't worry, you can change this. Philip Zimbardo and John Boyd, in their book *The Time Paradox*, found no evidence that time orientations are predetermined – we can change them.

'Grant me the serenity to accept the things I cannot change;

Courage to change the things I can;

And wisdom to know the difference.'

This is by the theologian Reinhold Niebuhr. Whether the spiritual aspect of this appeals to you or not, this remains one of the most powerful attitudes for how to manage your time.

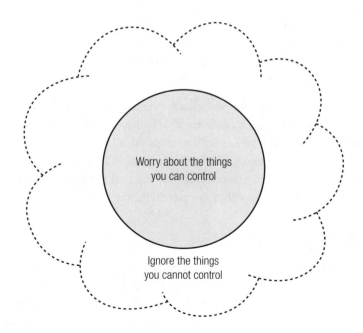

Worry about the things you can control

Ignore the things you cannot control

A balanced attitude to time

Past, present and future time orientations all have their advantages. Your aim should be to harness the positive elements of each one and to diminish the negative elements. Here are three techniques you can use to introduce this balance:

Detoxify your past

A strong positive attitude to your past will give you confidence in your future, so it's important if you do have a negative attitude to your past that you try to reduce this.

> a strong positive attitude to your past will give you confidence in your future

Your recollections of your past are entirely perception; the reality is long gone. Whenever you think about past events, focus on the good and, thinking of your mind's eye as a TV set, as you picture the happy moments, the small triumphs and the good relationships, allow yourself to turn up the volume, increase the brightness, make the colours more vivid and turn the image into wide-screen, high-definition, 3D format. If you catch yourself thinking about unhappy events or failures, let them fade away, dim and recede. Push them out and replace them with great outcomes.

brilliant exercise

Five ways to detoxify your past

- Think through some significant events in your life and, for each one, decide what the main benefit of them has been or can be for you.

- Think about people who have done you wrong and mentally forgive them. A great way to do this is to write down on a slip of paper the injustice you feel. Then, take all of those slips to a

▶

bin in the street and throw them away. Say to yourself: 'these injustices are in my past; they are gone.'

- Call someone you have lost touch with and tell them what you miss about having them as a friend. And call some people you are still in touch with and tell them how much you love and appreciate them. Start with anyone you live with.

- Start a gratitude journal and, each evening, write down one thing from that day that you are grateful for.

- Spend time with people who are positive about the past and optimistic about the future. Spending time with other people who complain about things and who are bitter about past events can only toxify your own life.

Tune in to the moment – become more present-oriented

If you have a strong past or future orientation and find yourself losing sight of the possible pleasures of now, in favour of a mad dash to get more and more done, allow yourself times when you live entirely in the present and savour every moment. For example, when you go out for dinner with a friend, try to really focus on the food that you eat; taste every mouthful. Listen carefully to what they have to say and spend time enjoying their company. Most importantly, don't worry about what time it is, how you are getting home, or what you have to do tomorrow – just focus on the pleasure of now.

One friend of mine did something startling at her party; she took off my watch. When you have no access to 'the time', then the only time that there is, is **now**.

> **brilliant** exercise
>
> **Five ways to tune in to the moment**
>
> ● Practise relaxation exercises like yoga, pilates or the Alexander technique.
>
> ● Be still for a period of time: for example, have a massage or meditate.
>
> ● Leave your watch at home.
>
> ● Stop what you are doing and go out for a walk.
>
> ● Take up a new and complex physical skill, like a martial art, a circus skill or a craft.

An eye to the future – become more future-oriented

If you are overly oriented to the present, start to focus on what you would like to achieve in the future by setting yourself goals and making plans. Chapter 4 will give you the resources you need to create goals for your life, but you can start more simply. Think of a project you have on at the moment; set aside half an hour to answer these seven simple questions.

1. What is the purpose of your project?
2. What will success look like?
3. What will it achieve when you have successfully completed it?
4. When do you *need* to have it completed, and when would you *like* to have it completed?
5. What are the principal steps in completing your project?
6. When do you want to complete each step?
7. When will you start each step and what is the next thing to do?

Keep a note of how the decisions you make and the things you do make changes to your life and the things around you; you have control.

brilliant exercise

Five ways to have more of an eye on the future

- Start to wear a watch and use a diary, if you do not already.

- Keep a note of how the decisions you make and the things you do make changes to your life and the things around you. This will demonstrate to you that you do have control.

- Write down what you want to achieve by the end of the month.

- Review all of your behaviours – diet, exercise, drinking, drugs, hygiene, risk-taking – and ask yourself what impact each will have on your life expectancy. Pick one thing to change, and do something different for the next month.

- Practise saying no to temptations and start offering yourself small rewards for when a job is completed – fully.

Can you change?

There is a wonderful Cherokee story about a tribal elder who is walking with his grandson.

'There is a fight going on inside of me,' he said to the boy. 'It has been raging since I was your age, and it is between two wolves. One wolf is evil; it is anger, envy, sorrow, regret, greed, arrogance, self-pity, guilt, resentment, inferiority, lies, false pride, superiority and ego. The other wolf is good; it is joy, peace, love, hope, serenity, humility, kindness, benevolence, empathy, generosity, truth, compassion and faith. This same fight will be going on inside of you – and inside every person.'

The grandson thought about it for a minute and then asked his grandfather: 'Which wolf will win?'

The old Cherokee simply replied, 'The wolf you feed.'

 **recap**

- If your primary orientation is towards the past, focus on the good memories and the benefits you gained from events – even the unpleasant ones. Dwelling on past failures, resentments and anger will poison your ability to create the future you want.

- A focus on the present can enable you to get lots done and enjoy the moment, but don't let it become a frenzy of meaningless activity, nor an indolent wait for something better to happen.

- If you have a strong orientation towards the future, you will be confident in your planning and diligent in getting things done. Avoid taking on too much and not benefitting from opportunities to relax and enjoy yourself.

- Only take on tasks that are within your control; don't dissipate your energy trying to achieve things that you have neither the resources nor the authority to complete.

- Create a balance in your life between different time orientations, so that you can gain the confidence of a strong positive attitude to your past, an enthusiasm to savour the moment, and a desire to control your future.

CHAPTER 2

Understand how you use your time

n the last chapter we looked at your attitude towards time and found that you have your own combination of past, present and future orientations. This will clearly have ramifications for the habits you have developed around how you use your time. So, in this chapter you will learn how to measure the way you do actually use your time.

In the spirit of the adage: 'what gets measured gets managed', this will help you to identify where your time goes and what the causes are for not getting done everything you want to do. Once you have this information, you will be able to identify which tools and techniques from *How to Manage Your Time* will best help you to manage your time.

This chapter is divided into two parts: we will start with how to calculate the value of your time, and then go on to look at how you can monitor where your time goes.

The value of your time

Calculating the value of your time in monetary terms is an easy sum to do, although to do it you must make some assumptions that are open to debate. So, if you don't agree with the assumptions in the examples in this section, do feel free to replace them with some of your own.

If you are employed

Our first decision is whether to look at the value of your time to your employer, or the cost of your time. If you are worth employing, the cost will be the more conservative, smaller number, so we will start with that.

The cost of employing you will include all of the charges, equipment and accommodation costs that are necessary for you to fulfil your role. Known as on-costs, these are typically from one-third to half of your salary in total. We will assume it is half of your salary.

Therefore, the cost of employing you for a year is about one-and-a-half times your salary. If you divide this number by the number of weeks you work in a year, and then divide again by the number of hours you work in a week, the answer is the cost, per hour, of your time.

Anita earns £20,000 per year and works 45 weeks, at 35 hours per week. Her time costs her employer:

$$\text{Cost per hour} = \frac{1.5 \times £20,000}{45 \times 35} = £19 \text{ per hour}$$

The value of Anita's time will depend on how much her job contributes to her employer's business and is much harder to calculate. Some businesses, however, charge their customers for staff time. In these cases the value is readily available.

If Anita's employer charges her clients £50 per hour for her time, then how Anita uses her time will be a matter of great interest to both her employer and her clients.

If you work for yourself

If you work for yourself, then the value of your time is your total income divided by the number of hours you work, and the cost of your time is your total fixed costs divided by the minimum number of hours you will be available to work. Bill's business costs him £18,000 a year to run, and he turned over £60,000 last year. He works 46 weeks a year and puts in around 52 hours a week.

The cost of his time is approximately £7.50 per hour, and the value is around £25 per hour.

When you are at leisure

When you are at leisure, you really ought not to be counting the cost!

However, you may sometimes want to do so, when making a decision. Let's say Charley wants to decide whether to pay a professional painter and decorator £100 to paint her bathroom, or do it herself. Her painter would take a day to prepare and paint the walls and charge her £100. She would probably take longer. How much is her time worth?

Assuming Charley has the spare cash, the answer lies in how long she would take to earn £100 of cash, after tax. Charley earns £30,000 per year and the tax office takes £10,000 of it. If she works 45 weeks, at 35 hours per week, it takes her 45 × 35 hours to earn £20,000 after tax. This equates to nearly £12.70 per hour, so it would take her between seven and eight hours to earn the £100.

So, all things being equal, Charley would pay the painter to do the work if it would take Charley over eight hours to do the work, and would do it herself if she could do it in under seven hours. If she thinks it will take her between seven and eight hours, then she will need another way to make her decision.

Cost or value?

When you are making decisions about how to allocate your time, always work on value. If you make decisions based on cost, you will never use your time to its full potential.

Where does your time go?

It is a common experience to sometimes find work left over at the end of the day. If this happens to you a lot, the first step is to understand where your time goes; you need to keep a time log. How long you need to keep it for is entirely dependent on how long it takes for you to spot patterns of behaviour and really understand what is driving your use of time. Typically, people with a reasonable amount of routine in their work pattern need to record three cycles of that routine.

A time log looks like the table below and you can download examples from **www.brilliant-timemanagement.com**.

Time Log				
Date:				
Time	Activity Description	Planned / Unplanned / Interrupted	Energy level Low / Med / High	Type of Activity
8.00				
8.20				
8.40				
9.00				
9.20				
9.40				

brilliant exercise

Throughout the working day, note your activities and the time you spend on them, as accurately as possible. This should include interruptions, conversations and breaks. Here is an example:

9.00–9.20   Check emails and chat with Danny
9.20–9.40   Draft two letters to service users
9.40–10.00   Telephone call from irate client – making file note

10.00–10.20   Start work on report
10.20–10.40   Work on report, chat with Hetal in tea room
10.40–11.00   More report – interrupted by telephone query

Make a note of whether each activity slot is planned, unplanned or has interrupted your plans, and record your energy levels throughout the day – high, medium or low. Also classify the types of activity you do in each time slot as A, B, C, etc:

A. Core role

B. Projects

C. Planning and thinking

D. Social and pleasure

E. Reactive response

F. Time wasting

What do your time logs tell you?

You may want to collate all of the information on a spreadsheet (and if you do, you can download a spreadsheet at **www.brilliant-timemanagement.com**). This will tell you precisely how much of your time you spend in different areas of work.

However, much of the value of your time log will be in a careful inspection.

● Do the proportions of time you spend on different types of activity seem about right?

● When do you most often get interrupted – and by what?

● When are the peaks and troughs of your energy – and what do you do then?

● What sort of things seem to trigger your peaks and troughs of energy?

- How much time do you spend on planned or unplanned activities?

- How much time do you spend in big blocks and how much is fragmented?

- How long do regular jobs take you – and how does it compare with the time you allow?

This information will help you spot tips and techniques later in this book which will particularly help you. Let's look at some examples.

I am constantly trying to juggle lots of different things
Multi-tasking is rarely as efficient as people think it is; in fact, recent research shows us that it can diminish how well you use your time. There is more on this in Chapter 5.

Interruptions constantly get in the way of doing things
If you know how to evaluate an interruption using the SCOPE process and you have some techniques to deal with time stealers, you can create a lot more productive time. There is more on this in Chapter 6.

I seem to get things started and then move on to other things
It is important to know when to keep going with a project, and when to let go of it. There is more on this in Chapter 7.

I spend a lot of my time doing things for other people that are not what I want to do for myself, or a part of my job or ...
On the face of it, this is simple: say 'no' more often. There is more on how to say 'no' in Chapter 8.

I seem to run out of energy at around ...
Knowing when you run out of energy will help you to understand your time cycles and so plan your activities accordingly. There is more on this in Chapter 10.

Jobs seem to take longer than I expected
You are probably either not planning well or, if you are planning, your estimating needs to improve. There is more on estimating in Chapter 10, and more on planning in Chapter 11.

Things seem to get done in a random order, with no sense of logic or priority
Planning is what will bring order and structure to your projects and activities. There is more on this in Chapter 11.

 brilliant recap

- Your time is worth money, so understand how much it is worth before you make decisions about what you do with it.

- Create a time log so that you can see how you are using your time and so identify what your time-management challenges really are.

CHAPTER 3

Six fundamentals of how to manage your time

Getting things done is rarely a problem when we feel passionately about what we do. It is at its most difficult when we face an unappealing task and we feel unmotivated and even resistant to doing it. This is when getting things done can become a challenge, and so you need to manage your time actively.

If you are overly present-oriented, you will hardly see the purpose in dealing with unpleasant matters – you will prefer either to do something more fun, or will take the pessimistic view of 'why bother – it won't change anything'. It is future-orientation that allows us to invest time doing things we'd rather not do, for a future benefit or to avoid a future penalty.

A proactive approach to getting things done

If we study how future-oriented people tackle tasks and projects, we consistently find that they take a proactive approach that allows them to take command of their affairs before their affairs take command of them. If you want to be in control of your time, this is a necessary first step, and here are the six fundamental principles that future-oriented people use.

1. Communication
2. Discipline
3. Memory

4. Planning

5. Review

6. Organisation

We will look at each of these in turn.

Number 1: Communication

One of the biggest wastes of your time can often be the consequences of either miscommunication or failure to communicate. Investing time in making sure you communicate well and in a timely fashion can reduce misunderstandings and failures of other people to do what you expect of them.

When someone asks you to do something, confirm back to them your understanding of what you are going to do and seek their agreement. When you set up a meeting, always confirm it in writing with a brief email. If you are coming up to a meeting that you arranged more than a week ago, send a reminder.

always take responsibility for your communication

The secret to good communication is simple: always take responsibility for your communication. Say to yourself: 'it is *my* job to ensure you understand what I am saying' and also 'it is *my* job to ensure I understand what you are saying'. This is hardly fair, but it will save you a lot of time and no little heartache in the long run.

Number 2: Discipline

Of all the habits that will help you succeed in managing your time, discipline is the most important. It will get you through the tough times and help you to build a valuable reputation. Discipline is about remembering what you must not forget, planning what must go well, reviewing what you must learn from and organising what must not get lost.

Discipline goes further than gritting your teeth and doing what you need to do. It is about being punctual, keeping your promises and remaining courteous and gracious under pressure. When you get these things right as a habit, people will start to grant you some leeway when things get difficult.

Discipline is rarely about doing things that are hard: it is more often about making the effort to do things that are easy, when you would really rather do nothing at all. And don't be tempted to think that discipline is only about the things you 'have to' do; often it takes discipline to stop doing those things and relax for a while.

brilliant tip

Establish routines that work. Once you practise a routine for long enough (between ten and twenty times, usually) it becomes habit. Now you will have a way to cope with your crisis next time.

Number 3: Memory

Punctuality does not just require discipline, it also requires planning, which we'll talk about in the next section, and memory. You may well be thinking 'but I have an awful memory' – it's quite a common belief. Never fear, there are three loaves of comfort – crumbs are for the truly impoverished.

1. You have a phenomenal memory. If you are not getting the best out of it, then the major reason will be that you just don't care enough about the things you forget. How many people forget their child's name – even after they have just named him or her? And if you really don't care, but need to remember anyway ... file that conundrum under D for 'discipline'.

2. There are a stack of methods to help you use your memory effectively and an even bigger stack of books on the market to tell you how. I forget how many.

3. You don't even need your memory. Modern-day humans have invented all sorts of tools to supplement the 1.1 kilos of organic matter our ancestors had to rely upon. You can have everything from notepads to iPads.

Your memory will help you to get done the things that you need to do before they become so pressing that you feel you have no control over them and that they are starting to take over your life. When you lose perspective like this, even the simplest of tasks can seem over-bearing. Worse still, if you do not remember to do certain things, then the consequences can be unpleasant.

Number 4: Planning

Planning is the mark of the proactive person. Figuring out in advance what you are going to do, and when, puts you right in the centre of events with the best chance of controlling them. Notice, however, that this is not the same as suggesting that if you have a plan, you will be 'in control' of events.

General (later President) Dwight David Eisenhower said: 'In preparing for battle I have always found that plans are useless, but planning is indispensable.' You will notice that the universe often has a habit of kicking your plans up the backside and then laughing at you. But, as Eisenhower observed, it is the process of planning that prepares you to understand what is going on and what your options are. When you can combine effective planning with flexible responses, you are in the prime position to manage your time in any circumstances. We'll cover planning in more detail in Chapter 11.

> it is the process of planning that prepares you to understand what is going on

Number 5: Review

'Keep working at it and it will work out okay in the end' is the sort of wisdom repeated by parents and guardians up and down the country. Sadly, it is not always true. This approach leads to a blinkered focus on what is immediately before you and can lead to you missing the ten-ton truck coming at you from the left.

Far better to take breaks and:

- review your progress;
- review your priorities;
- review your successes;
- review your failures;
- review your process.

Heads up, polish your binoculars, take a look around, then onto the next step.

Number 6: Organisation

Being organised may not save you time, but it will allow you to use the time you have well, and look forward to tasks without that foreboding sense of 'it's such a mess'. An important part of being organised is being tidy, but it is important to apply your own sort of 'tidy'.

Some people need regimented neatness, while others like their work space to be a Spartan blank slate, and yet others need the cosy familiarity of their own objects filling their space – what to anyone else would seem like clutter. However you like your work space, regularly make time to organise it.

---

brilliant example

The old saying goes: 'A place for everything and everything in its place'.

It is no coincidence that professionals in many disciplines have systems for organising the tools of their trade; whether it is the systematic sequencing of a surgeon's instruments so that theatre staff can find what they need instantly, or the shadow boards that always store tools in an engineering ▶

workshop on a wall to keep surfaces clear, with a painted silhouette of each tool so gaps are immediately obvious, as is each tool's home.

Keeping tidy

For many of us our most valuable tool is our desk (whether you work from home or in an office). If this is the case with you, try to keep your desk as tidy as you can manage and remove everything that you are not currently working on. If you have several projects, then gather the books and papers for each project into a pile, a file, or a box and find it a location in a drawer or cupboard, on a shelf, or, if you are comfortable with this, on a patch of floor.

If you have a workshop or work-room where you build, repair or make things, the same principle will apply. You need to know where all of your tools, supplies and materials are so you can access them quickly, and you need to have your projects conveniently grouped, and out of the way, so that the project you are working on now will not be hindered by the clutter of another on-going activity.

For some people, clearing their space is more than a good habit, it's a necessity. I am not talking here about people working in a secure environment or who work on confidential or valuable data; I mean people for whom visual clutter is a terrible distraction. If you are like this, you will recognise the feeling of almost frozen inaction when faced with a disordered, over-full desk or work space. Deal with it immediately, or face a period of procrastination and slow working.

Other people like the comfort of a cluttered environment. If you are like this, then you will find yourself somewhere on the following scale.

● Your 'clutter' may look random to me, but it has a very distinct pattern to you. You can find what you need quickly and easily and you have just enough space to do the work you need to do. Everything else is neither a distraction nor inconvenience.

- Your clutter is indeed random. You cannot find anything and waste a lot of time looking. When you do find what you need you cannot work efficiently because the other stuff gets in your way.

If you are towards the top end of that scale, then keep your clutter: it works for you. But if you are just kidding yourself and you know that the clutter is killing your productivity, then it is time to do something about it.

brilliant tip

You'll find plenty of books recommending the layout of a workstation, but there is no substitute for knowing your habits and workload and ensuring that the things you need often are easily in reach and the things you don't need often are stored out of the way. However, there is one absolute 'must' that I learned the hard and very painful way.

Always ensure that what you are working on at any time is square on to where you sit and straight ahead of you. Too many books show, for example, a computer screen neatly placed in that dead corner of the desk. It is great for optimum use of space, but awful for your posture. Nothing will spoil your time-management plans more than two weeks of agonising back pain. So, ergonomics first; then convenience; then aesthetics.

Organised filing

Who would declare filing to be their favourite job? Love it or loathe it, a good system, applied with discipline, will serve you well. Here are a range of helpful tips.

Your process

When paperwork comes your way, call PAT. There are three things that you can do; you can either:

● Pass it on – to someone better able to deal with it;

● Act on it – in your own time, then file it;

● Throw it away – file it in the round filing cabinet on the floor.

Always do the filing on current projects immediately, so you can find things when you need them. All other filing is most economically done in batches. Create a 'to-be-filed' tray to collect papers that you need to file, and then do the filing once a week, once a month or quarterly, according to the volumes of papers you gather.

Your system

One simple system, used by everyone, will be far more valuable than a complex 'perfect' system that few use and even fewer use properly. As with much in life, keep it simple. Here are two simple approaches to filing that may work well for you, if you don't already have your own.

Simple system number one: proximity filing. Every time you remove a file from a shelf or drawer, return it to the most accessible end of the shelf, or the front of the drawer. This way you will soon find you rarely have to go far to get a file or folder.

Simple system number two: chronological filing. If each file covers a single topic, then put papers into it in date order with the newest at the front where they are easy to find. When the file is full, start volume two and you have the other one ready to archive.

If your current system doesn't work and you want to change it, don't start by re-filing all of your historic papers. This could be a lot of abortive work. Instead, create your new system and only file old papers into it when you access them. That way old papers you don't access will work their way to archiving in a functional (even if sub-optimal) filing system.

Your files

Label all of your files clearly and prominently. Some people also like colour-coding, while others like pictures, but what is most important is that the contents of each folder, file or box are completely obvious without having to open it.

Small current projects can sit nicely in clear plastic slip folders. Create a template file front sheet for these (download examples at **www.brilliant-timemanagement.com**) onto which you can write the file name and any key data. When you are working on a project it often pays to type up a 'key information sheet' to go into the front of your file. Update it by hand and, from time to time, type up amendments and print an updated version.

If you like keeping magazine articles and snippets from papers, keep a cuttings file. An easy way to do this is to get a scrapbook or A4 bound notebook and paste the articles in. You can now annotate them with your thoughts. If you want to find things easily, rather than try and think of a total classification scheme at the outset, label pages as you go and create an index at the back.

If you keep lots of notebooks, it is a good idea to number them and always put your name and phone number on the front page, so if you lose it there is a chance it will be returned. If you think you will want to refer to material in them, it might be a good idea to number each page, so that you can refer to the meeting notes at 3–57 – page 57 of notebook number 3.

Buying an organiser

Paper and electronic organisers can be brilliant and there are a wealth of options to try out. And that is exactly what you should do; invest some time in trying a few out, one at a time, for two or three weeks each. Get to experience what you like and don't like about each one and decide what sort of organiser (or none) is right for you. Then go looking for one that most nearly meets your specifications. As you go through this book, make a note (in the margin, on sticky notes or in a notebook) of ideas that strike you as useful for *your* ideal organiser.

brilliant recap

● Good communication will prevent time-wasting misunderstandings.

● Discipline comes from an inner resolve to do something, regardless of what you would rather be doing.

● Remember to do the things you need to do, and to be punctual. You can either choose to train your memory with powerful techniques, or use tools like notebooks, diaries or computers to help you.

● Effective time managers plan what they are going to do, and then review the outcomes, so that they can plan more effectively next time.

● Be organised by keeping things tidy and getting an efficient system for your filing.

CHAPTER 4

Know what you are doing things for

Whatever time orientation you have, whether past, present or future, you still need a reason to do things. It is not just children who ask 'why' when told to do something, adults do it too; we just do it differently. Sometimes, the 'why' stays in our head and sabotages our progress. The two things that will motivate you to get on and do something are wanting to do it and understanding why it is necessary or important. When you have a strong reason for doing something, because you can see the meaning or purpose of it, then you can commit to it. Then getting it done will no longer seem like a chore – no matter how unpleasant it is. Instead, it will feel like a mission.

when you have a strong reason for doing something, then you can commit to it

Future-oriented people know what they want to achieve, have, or be, and work towards it. The tool they use is goal setting. This chapter is about how to set goals that will be your basis for committing to future actions. You will be able to go back to your time log and review how much of your time is spent on activities that will move you towards your goals. Then, as you move through the rest of this book, you will learn time-management techniques that will allow you to achieve your goals.

The four sections in this chapter cover: the importance of goals and why they work; getting started in goal-setting with goals at different levels – goals for your life, for a year, and for shorter terms; how to state your goals in a powerful way; and how to discover what your ultimate goals really are.

 example

The Harvard – or Yale – goal-setting study myth

If you read enough self-help books, or attend enough seminars, you are bound to eventually come across the '1979 Harvard Goal-setting Study' or the '1953 Yale Goal-setting Study'. In these studies, a team of researchers interviewed graduating students and asked them whether they had written down the specific goals for their life. Years later the researchers tracked them all down and found that the 3 per cent of people who had specific goals at the start of the study had accumulated more personal wealth than the other 97 per cent of their classmates combined. The study is often quoted to illustrate the power of focus.

There is just one tiny problem – recent researchers have looked for evidence and found that neither experiment actually took place.

The good news is that Professor Gail Matthews, a psychologist at Dominican University of California has done a similar experiment, looking at factors which enhance achievement of business- and work-related goals. On her website (**www.dominican.edu/duoc_edu/academics/ahss/ psych/faculty/fulltime/gailmatthews**) she describes an experiment where 149 students were asked to set and pursue goals in one of five different ways. After four weeks, they were asked to rate the degree to which they had accomplished their goals. Professor Matthews reports an average goal-achievement score of 4.3 for students with no written goals and 6.4 for students with written goals.

The importance of goals

Goals guide you and set the direction of all your actions. Without goals, your time management can only ever be reactive to events and requests from other people. Perhaps most importantly, if you don't have goals you won't ever know when you are successful, so you will never feel a true sense of achievement and fulfilment.

Goals are about optimism, not a blind faith that everything will be okay in the end, but a positive belief that says 'I know what I want, I am confident that the opportunities I need are out there, and I will seize those opportunities when they arise.'

Why goals work

Inside your head is a small part of your brain called the Reticular Activating System (RAS). Its function seems to be like a child's toy that has different-shaped holes in it, to accommodate different-shaped pegs. When you prime your RAS with something you want to spot, it surveys your environment constantly and, as soon as it spots something relevant, it alerts you. You might call it instead your 'serendipity organ'. Once you know what your goals are, your serendipity organ will spot opportunities that will help you achieve them.

How do you know this works? Because most people have had the experience of getting a new car and noticing for the first time how many there are on the road, over the next few days. Or wearing a new watch or piece of jewellery for the first time and being constantly worried about it. All this is caused by your serendipity organ being primed to notice your model of car, or the new feeling of your watch or jewellery.

What are goals?

Goals answer the question: 'What do I want?'

They set out your aims in life and what you consider to be success and fulfilment. Once you have your goals clear in your mind, they will guide you as much about what not to do as about what to do, so they will not only help you to focus on what really matters to you, but they will also help you screen out the inconsequential diversions that will steal your time from you.

Starting your goal-setting

We will look at goals for your life, for a year, and for shorter terms.

Your Life Will

It is helpful to think about wills. A will is a conscious choice or an expression of a desire or a wish.

A will sets out what you want to happen when you die. Some people also have a 'living will', which sets out what they want to happen if they become terminally ill. However, let's focus on the rest of your life; why not also create a 'Life Will'?

Your Life Will sets out your desires and wishes for your life: what you want to have, achieve, experience. Like a normal will, you should review it from time to time as your life and circumstances change. This becomes the guiding document for your life and, each year, you can set out some annual goals to guide and motivate you through your year. You can download a Life Will form from **www.brilliant-timemanagement.com** or simply write down your life goals somewhere that is safe and private to you.

brilliant exercise

Discover what to put into your Life Will

Life is a journey, and this exercise will take you on that journey in your mind. There are other exercises to complement this one later in this chapter. You will need a lined notepad or notebook and pen or pencil. Before you start, mark six pages in your pad with the headings:

- My whole life – what do I want?
- Ten years into my future life – what do I notice?
- Three years into my future life – what do I notice?
- One year into my future life – what do I notice?
- Six months into my future life – what do I notice?
- Three months into my future life – what do I notice?

Find yourself somewhere comfortable to sit, where you will not be disturbed for half an hour to an hour. Sit down and gradually, once you are comfortable, allow your eyes to close and start to picture your whole life. What do you want to achieve? What experiences do you want? What do you want to acquire?

Now picture your life in ten years' time. Where are you, who are you with, what are you doing? Explore your perfect life in ten years' time, visualising as much detail as you want and noticing how you have changed and what you have achieved. Take from five to ten minutes to do this, exploring every aspect of your life: your work, your family, and you, yourself.

When you have finished, open your eyes and, in your own time, make a note of all of the important events and achievements you noticed, along with the qualities of your life in ten years' time.

Once you have finished making your list, get up and have a stretch, before returning to your seat, closing your eyes, and visualising your life in three years' time. Repeat the procedure of mentally exploring your life and then writing down what you notice, what you have done and what you have experienced for three years, one year, six months and three months.

What you have noted down at the end of this exercise is your Life Will.

Your annual goals

Each year, set aside some time to think through what the coming year will be all about for you; what things you want to achieve and what steps you plan to take to achieve them. A great time to do this is in the days between the Christmas holiday and New Year, although any time during January works very well.

> set aside some time to think through what the coming year will be all about for you

There is something special to human beings about beginnings, and, in our culture, the start of the calendar year is a powerful beginning. One likely reason for this extends beyond the convention of our calendar to the recognition that days are now slowly starting to get longer and spring is on its way, with the new life it brings.

If you have missed this opportunity, don't worry: there are plenty more. There are beginnings throughout the year: your birthday, the start of spring, autumn time – when some cultures celebrate their new year, linked to harvest time. There are also the starts of months or weeks, or even when *you choose* to start the rest of your life.

Set your goals for the year in four tiers:

Tier 1: Theme

It is a nice idea to give each year a 'theme' which sets out your main focus for the year. This does not mean that you won't set goals in other areas, but it does answer the question: 'what do I really want to make happen this year to take my life to the next step?' Here are some examples from my own annual goals, to illustrate the term theme.

1999   Career – promotion

2000   Relationships

2001	New home
2002	Career – change
2003	Stabilisation
2004	Business growth
2005	Local community

An interesting observation is that, in each of these years, I made major changes to my life in these directions. However, in 2006 my theme was overtaken by two huge opportunities in the early months, which I chose to work on. They consumed all of my energy and yet, when I look back at that theme, I can see how both opportunities have helped me achieve the change I wanted – only some time later, in 2009 and 2010.

Tier 2: Big goals

Set yourself from two to five big goals for what you want to achieve this year. What do you want to be different in a year's time? What do you want to have experienced or achieved? Some of these should be linked to your theme, but you may want some other changes too.

Tier 3: Detailed goals

Examine each area of your life and set between three and seven detailed goals for things you want to do, experience, or change in that specific area.

📐 brilliant tool

A Balance Wheel will give you an idea of how to balance your detailed goals across the different areas of your life. The wheel overleaf is like a pizza with six different toppings:

Myself – your health and fitness, your spiritual life, recreation and the contribution you make to the people and society around you.   ▶

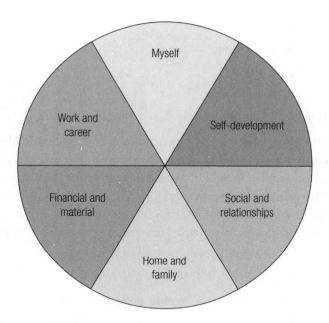

Self-development – how you want to change yourself, by learning, growing and expanding your mind.

Social and relationships – who you want to be in contact with and how you want to develop your relationships. The social life you want and your place in your community.

Home and family – your home life and the way you want to develop your home and your relationships with your family. The part you want to play in the hopes and aspirations of close family members.

Financial and material – your assets and finances and how you want to manage your affairs; this includes aspirations for debt and savings.

Work and career – what you want to do and achieve in the world of work, and how you want to progress your career.

Create your own pizza toppings by deciding what are the principal areas of your life.

Tier 4: Urgent priorities

There may be no urgent priorities, but take some time to think through what you need to work on if you are going to achieve the rest of your goals. For example, if you are unfit, this can compromise your ability to work on your goals effectively, so you may set priorities around exercise or diet. Alternatively, if you have too much debt this may be diverting your attention from other, positive and progressive, goals, so reducing or clearing that debt may be your urgent priority.

Urgent priorities are the things you need to deal with in order to create the space you need to focus on your real goals. Set yourself the objective of working on all of your urgent priorities in the first quarter of the year ahead, leaving you three-quarters in which to achieve the things that matter most to you.

Short-term goals

Short-term goals are the outcomes that you set yourself on a monthly, weekly or daily basis and, as we will see in Chapter 10, they form the starting point of the ultimate process for how to manage your time. There are two ways in which you can form your short-term goals: from the top, downwards; or from the ground, upwards.

Top-down short-term goals

Setting your short-term goals from the top down means starting with your long-term goals and looking at the progress that you want to make on each one, in the relevant time span. So if you are setting yourself weekly goals, for example, you can follow these four steps:

1. **Review your life goals, the content of your Life Will**.
   Are there any opportunities available to you now that will allow you to pursue one of these goals? If so, create a short-term goal to capitalise on that opportunity.

2. **Is there a theme for this week?** Think about whether there is an area of your life, from your Balance Wheel, that you want to focus on this week. This will frame your thinking; it may suggest some outcomes that you'd like to pursue this week, and it will certainly help you to review your annual goals in steps 3 and 4.

3. **Review your Tier 4 goals, your urgent priorities for the year.** If there are any of those that you must or can make progress on, then you will probably want to include some short-term goals around them.

4. **Review your Tier 2 and 3 goals, your goals for the year.** Which ones of these do you want to focus on this week? Choose a small number of outcomes that will take you towards achieving them.

Bottom-up short-term goals

If you prefer to set your short-term goals from the ground upwards, there are two approaches:

Approach 1: If you have a 'to-do list' of things you have been meaning to get done, review this list and identify which tasks you want to achieve in the coming week. Set yourself goals around achieving clusters of tasks and making progress with particular projects that you have had in mind for a while, or that are already on-going.

Approach 2: Start with a blank sheet of paper and an open mind. Then make a list of everything you want to be different at the end of the coming week – whether it is things you would like to have achieved, changes to relationships, or progress on projects. Use this thought process as the basis for setting yourself specific goals.

How to state your goals in a powerful way

You may have come across the term 'SMART goals'. SMART reminds you to make your personal work objectives robust, and most commonly stands for Specific–Measurable–Achievable– Relevant–Timed. There are many variants on SMART, or even SMARTER, goals.

To get the best results, you will want to go one better and create the SMARTEST goals you can, by working really hard at thinking them through with great care and precision. SMARTEST stands for: Specific, Meaningful, Action-oriented, Responsible, Towards, Exciting, Supported, Time-bound. Here is what I mean by each of these words.

Specific

Make each objective as specific as you can. A great way to do this is to ask what, precisely, will be different when you have achieved it? Make it compelling by using language about what you would see, hear and feel when you have achieved your objective and, where possible, make it quantitative. Write your objectives as positive statements: 'I will …'

Meaningful

You will only be motivated to achieve objectives that you see as worthwhile, significant and relevant to your life goals or the context in which you are setting them. Humans need to see a purpose or else we will not be motivated to do something. To help you articulate this, start by writing down: 'I have set this goal because …'

> humans need to see a purpose or else we will not be motivated to do something

Action-oriented

Make sure that each objective is dependent upon you, rather than having a passive reliance on other people or events. This will give you a sense of control. Your objectives must be ones that you have initiated and that you can make happen, otherwise you risk feeling frustrated by a lack of luck. Luck has little or no part to play in achieving an action-oriented goal.

Responsible

You also need to believe that you are being responsible and ethical in pursuing your objectives: they must do no harm to you or others. Check that they fit within your own moral code and the rules and laws you have signed up to as a part of your community and a member of your organisation, otherwise your conscience will conflict with your goals and you will get into a 'lose-lose' trap. If you achieve your goal, you will feel bad: if your conscience succeeds in blocking it, you will feel frustrated by your failure. Also, make sure you believe that your goals are achievable; if not, you will find yourself devoting your life to a fantasy.

Towards

Choose positive, affirmative objectives that take you towards something worthwhile. If, instead, you word your objectives in terms of what you do not want ('I want to lose X', or '... get rid of Y'), you will find that you are overly focused on the negatives in your life. Even if X and Y are reducing, you will not feel good because you will continue to notice how much of them you still have. It is always easy to say what you don't want; so instead, look for the opposite of X or Y and say instead what you *do* want.

Exciting

Choose objectives that excite and challenge you. Look to achieve things that are enjoyable and rewarding. Under 'responsible', we said your objectives should be achievable; but they should not be too easily achievable or you will feel no sense of achievement when you succeed. The best goals are ones that stretch you.

Supported

Who and what can help you achieve your objectives? Sometimes you can be entirely self-sufficient, but often it pays to look for people to help you. You are not alone in the world, so inventory the support that is available to you. You may also need to get your objectives agreed by someone with the right level of authority (like your boss). Make sure you can get sign-off from anyone you need it from.

Time-bound

Set a target date for each objective and also interim review points to help track your progress, re-evaluate your approach, and keep you motivated. Sometimes it will help you to include interim objectives too. If your goals are not time-bound, then, when years have gone by with no progress, your unconscious brain will have no reason to put pressure on you: 'there's still time'.

How to discover what your goals really are

Discovering what goals you want to set and creating your Life Will can be difficult. This section offers you two ways to get underneath your conscious thinking and help you to understand what you really want for yourself. You can do each of them on your own, or you may want to work with a friend asking you the questions as you go through the process.

Your personal timeline

You will need a comfortable space where you will not be disturbed for around fifteen minutes. A living room with furniture pushed back to the walls is ideal. You will also need a set of markers to indicate different points on your timeline, labelled Now, 5 Years, 10 Years, 20 Years, My Death, 500 Years. You can download a set from **www.brilliant-timemanagement.com**.

1. Find a route along the floor for your timeline and lay out your markers on the ground, from your birth to 500 years from now.

2. Step onto your timeline at the Now position.

3. Turn with your back to the timeline and face your past. Close your eyes and notice all of the significant events in your life up to now. Make a mental inventory of all or some of the things that have made you who you are now.

4. When you are ready, turn around and face your future. Notice the position 500 years from now.

5. Walk along your timeline to the 500 Years position and turn back to face now. Close your eyes and notice what you see, hear and feel. What does your life mean from this vantage point?

6. When you are ready, open your eyes and move back along your timeline to the time of your physical death. Close your eyes and notice what you see, hear and feel. Notice all that you have achieved. What was your life all about? What did you do that you are most proud of? Imagine you can eavesdrop at your funeral; what are people saying about you? Listen in to the details. Get a sense of what matters most.

7. When you are ready, open your eyes and move to 20 Years from now. Close your eyes and notice what you see, hear and feel. Notice all that you have achieved. What changes did you make in these 20 years? Who are the people that are around you? Where are you now? What have you done that you are most proud of?

8. When you are ready, open your eyes and move to 10 Years from now. Close your eyes and notice what you see, hear and feel. Notice all that you have achieved. Where are you in 10 years? What has changed in the 10 years from now? What is most significant about this position?

9. When you are ready, open your eyes and move to 5 Years from now. Close your eyes and notice what you see, hear and feel. Notice all that is different and all that is the same. What are these five years all about? What do you most want to achieve?

10. When you are ready, open your eyes and move to Now. Turn and face your future. Close your eyes and notice how all the events realign themselves to support your vision, mission and purpose. What do you now recognise that you did not understand before?

When you are ready, open your eyes and step off your timeline. Now is a good time to sit down quietly and make a few notes about what you have learned.

Your mental levels

Allow at least fifteen minutes to do this exercise. Lay out a set of markers for each level on the floor, with at least 30cm between them. Label the markers: Environment, Behaviours, Capabilities, Identity, Purpose, Beliefs and Values. You can download a set from **www.brilliant-timemanagement.com**.

Choose an area of your life you would like to explore, knowing that at the least you will experience some new insight into it, and at best you might transform your experience of it.

1. When you are ready, step into the first space marked 'Environment'. Notice what you see, hear and feel as you are at your very best. Where are you when you engage in this area of your life? What do you see and hear? Who else is there with you?

2. When you are ready, step into the second space, marked 'Behaviours'. Seeing yourself in this environment, what specifically are you doing when you are at your most excellent? What do you do when you engage in this area of your life? What activities do you engage in? What strengths do you have? If someone were watching you on a video, what would they see you do? What would they hear you say?

3. When you are ready, step into the third space, marked 'Capabilities'. Seeing yourself in this environment, doing those things, what skills are you using that make you excellent? What capabilities do you tap into in this area of your life? What skills do you put into practice? What areas of expertise do you draw on? What other skills do you need, and what skills would be useful? Who do you know who has these?

4. When you are ready, step into the space marked 'Beliefs and Values'. What is important about this area of your life? Why does it matter? Why do you want to use these capabilities in this area of your life? What do you know to be true about this area of your life? What would be the most important thing for someone you love to know about it? Are there any other beliefs and values that would be useful to you (to guide your heart)?

   Complete the following sentences:
   ● 'The reality of [this topic] is …'
   ● 'The most important thing about [this topic] is …'

5. When you are ready, step forward into the space marked 'Identity'. Who are you when you are at your best in this area of your life? What do your beliefs and values, and capabilities and behaviours say about you? What metaphor best represents the kind of excellent person you are?

6. Finally, when you are ready, step into the space of
   'Purpose'. Close your eyes and take as long as you like to
   connect with the best and highest thing you can imagine
   – something beyond anything you have been exploring,
   whether you think of that as your god, your highest self,
   your connection with others, or how it all connects with
   the big picture of your life. What is your mission in life?
   Who else and what else are you serving when you are at
   your very best?

7. When you are ready, turn and face back down the way you
   came. Bringing all that you have seen, heard and felt with
   you, step into the space marked 'Identity'. Once again, who
   are you in this area of your life? Notice how your identity is
   enriched and enhanced by all that you have experienced.

8. Bringing your sense of purpose and your new or
   heightened sense of identity with you, step into the space
   of 'Beliefs and Values'. What is true about this area of
   your life? What is important about it? Why does it matter?
   Notice how your beliefs and values are enriched and
   enhanced by all that you have experienced.

9. Carrying your sense of purpose, your identity, and an
   awareness of your beliefs and values with you, step back
   into the space of your capabilities and skills. What new
   or additional capabilities and skills are you aware of that
   you draw on (or could draw on) in this area of your life?
   Notice how your capabilities are enriched and enhanced
   by all that you have experienced.

10. Still steeped in your sense of purpose, identity, beliefs,
    values and capabilities, step back into the space of your
    behaviours. What do you do or could you do in this area
    of your life? How have your behaviours changed? How
    have they stayed the same? What new things occur to you?
    Notice how your opportunities are enriched and enhanced
    by all that you have experienced.

11. Finally, take everything you have learned and experienced along the way back into the space of environment. Where are you? What do you see? What do you hear? Who else is there with you? Who is no longer there? Take all the time you need to notice everything that has changed. What specific differences have you noticed?

Allow all that you have learned and all of the changes you have made to settle in. You may like to make some notes of what you learned and experienced, and you may find the changes and insights continue to come for hours and sometimes days afterwards.

 **brilliant** recap

- Goals give you something to commit to, to motivate you, and to guide your decisions.

- Don't just make a will for when you are dead: make a Life Will to express your wishes for the life you want.

- Create annual goals each year, so that you know how to prioritise the things you could be doing during the coming twelve months.

- Put detail on your goals with objectives, and make them the SMARTEST they can be.

- Discover your goals with two powerful techniques: your personal timeline and your mental levels.

PART 2

Work effectively and avoid the pitfalls that steal your time

P art 2 of *How to Manage Your Time* is where you will get the tools you need to solve particular time-management problems. These can be summarised as:

I can't work effectively

Chapter 5 shows you how to work effectively, by avoiding too much multi-tasking, making effective choices about how to handle a task, and dealing with stress – which can sap your energy and rob you of your ability to work effectively. In addition, you will learn how to be effective in meetings and how to read effectively.

My problem is priorities

Chapter 6 will give you the tools that you need to set priorities and to enforce them, by dealing with the interruptions and time stealers that can otherwise override them.

I need to focus better

Chapter 7 is all about focus: its value, when to focus and when to stop, and the special times when you can really focus and get more done than you may have ever imagined.

I seem to do more for everyone else than I do for me

If your problem is saying 'no', Chapter 8 will show you how to do it with confidence and good grace.

CHAPTER 5

How to
do things
effectively

This chapter is fundamentally about how you can get the greatest possible amount done in the time you have available. For many people this means multi-tasking, but, as we will see, this is a poor solution and trying to do too much at a time can harm your efficiency.

The real solutions are to choose well how you respond to a task, and to have effective strategies for doing what you do. So this chapter we will pick up on some of the themes you read about in Chapter 3; in particular: planning, review and organisation.

There are six sections in this chapter, each looking at a different way in which you can get more done.

1. The balance between trying hard to get as much done as possible, and the desire to focus on one thing only and get it just right. We shall refer to these two personality types as the Octopus (with its eight hands each doing different things) and the Elephant (with its one precision hand).

2. In 'the multi-tasking fallacy' we will understand what multi-tasking is and why it reduces, rather than increases, your effectiveness.

3. In a section on making choices we will learn how the key to effectiveness is in making the right choices about what to do about the multitude of tasks you face. This will give you five approaches to any task.

4. The section on effective meetings offers you some tips and tools for how to make huge time savings in meetings.

5. When you transform the way you read, you can become more effective at gathering information quickly.

6. We will close the chapter by looking at stress, how its effects can damage your effectiveness, and how to regain control.

 brilliant definition

MILE stands for Maximum Impact for Least Effort.

Make sure you go miles better.

Elephant and Octopus personality types

The trunk of an African elephant is like a piece of precision engineering with between 40,000 and 150,000 separate muscles. It has two finger-like muscles at the end that the elephant can use to grab small items – Asian elephants have only one. Elephants focus on one thing at a time and take great care to get it right.

Octopuses are thought to be the most intelligent of all invertebrates. They have eight arms, each capable of almost independent thought, with the basic controls for voluntary movement embedded within the nerve system of the arm itself. With their exceptional problem-solving skills, octopuses can take on many tasks at once.

Are you an Elephant or an Octopus?

Take our Brilliant Quiz to estimate your propensity for focusing on one thing, or many. The number you get at the end will be a fun indication of the number of arms you need, from one for an Elephant personality to eight for the Octopuses among us.

⭐ brilliant quiz

Ⓠ Are you an Elephant or an Octopus?

First score your attitudes 0, 1 or 2 if you rarely, sometimes or often ...

❑ Take your time

❑ Feel fine if others do better

❑ Brush off frustrations

❑ Do one thing at a time

❑ Plan and prepare carefully

❑ Enjoy a well-earned break

❑ Take it steady and do it well

Total Elephant score _____

Now score your attitudes 0, 1 or 2 if you rarely, sometimes or often ...

❑ Mustn't be late

❑ Feel highly competitive

❑ Get impatient

❑ Do lots of things at once

❑ Work 'just in time'

❑ Feel guilty when you relax

❑ Rush to hit deadlines

Total Octopus score _____

❑ Subtract your Elephant score from your Octopus score _____

❑ Add 18 to get a number between 4 and 32 _____

❑ Divide by 4 to get a number between 1 and 8 _____

The danger with being an Elephant is that you can get fixated on one task and lose all track of time. Elephants like to relax, but they can frustrate the people around them with their laid-back attitude. Octopuses, on the other hand, tend to rush around trying to get as much done as possible; watching them can be exhausting. Because they are trying to accomplish so much, there is always the risk that something important can get missed. Remarkably, however, most Octopuses seem to always get the job done, but with not a moment to spare.

Few of us are as extreme as the Elephant or the Octopus, but if you recognise some of the traits in yourself, let's look at how each can adapt its style.

Herding the Elephant

An Elephant can be equally happy engrossed in filing or a vital report. Whichever it is, they tend to work hard to get things absolutely right. Often they like detail and hate sudden change, so to harness their strengths, Elephants need to ensure that they make plans that allow everything to be programmed into their day, so that perfection becomes working to the plan, not perfecting one task. However, their dislike of sudden changes means that they can be inflexible, and a plan can exacerbate this, so a wise Elephant will ensure that they plan contingency time into their day, to handle the unexpected events. Another of their strengths is their ability to think deeply about things, so Elephants need to schedule good-quality thinking time so that they do not feel rushed into the decisions they must make.

Elephants are often a pleasure to speak with because they get lost in the conversation and become oblivious to time. This can make them late for the next meeting – which they really don't mind. But other people around them do mind, so Elephants are well served by the timed reminder functions on many portable devices.

Taming the Octopus

Octopuses sometimes need nothing more than to slow down. They have great difficulty saying 'no', so they accumulate tasks and responsibilities which they feel obliged to deliver upon. Often this means rushed work that is never quite finished, because of their dual need to get it done in time and also to stay stimulated. So at the extremes of this personality they hand over shoddy work. Even if they had the time, the finishing touches would bore them. To work around this, the shrewd Octopus will plan well in advance and set early deadlines to avoid last-minute rushes. They will also split up tasks, so that the final touches become a new challenge.

Relaxing is a problem for an Octopus, because they feel that they always have to be doing something – and often two things, or three. They like to take their meals quickly, while reading a book or a magazine, and with the radio or television on in the background.

Unlike Elephants, Octopuses are acutely aware of time. When speaking with people, they can show their boredom, frustration or desire to move on to the next thing. This can alienate the person they are speaking with, so a powerful technique is for the Octopus to set themselves objectives for each conversation that compels them to listen hard.

The multi-tasking fallacy

Multi-tasking is doing more than one thing at the same time. Study after study and, if we are honest with ourselves, everyday experience, too, confirms that as the number of tasks we are working on increases, the quality and quantity of our work diminishes. In this section we are going to try to understand why this is. We will consider first whether multi-tasking is possible, then the three problems multi-taskers have, and finally we will ask what the conditions for peak performance are.

Multi-tasking – is it possible?

A body of evidence suggests that there are two distinct circumstances to consider, if we want to know if multi-tasking is
possible. To illustrate these, let us start with the simplest form
of multi-tasking: doing two things at once. Here are the two
circumstances: first, one task is taxing or novel, and the other is
highly familiar; and second, both tasks are taxing or novel.

The taxing or novel tasks require conscious concentration, such
as planning or problem-solving, while the familiar tasks can be
done almost unconsciously. For many of us this includes driving,
walking, or listening to music. When we first encountered these,
though, they were novel and demanded our conscious attention.
You may not remember when, as a newly toddling infant, you
had to concentrate on every step, but most drivers remember
having to figure out each time which sequence of pedals and how
much pressure were needed to change gear smoothly.

When multi-tasking is and is not possible

So, back to the two circumstances: in the first, when one task
is taxing or novel and the other is highly familiar, we do seem
to be able to carry out both actions together. Our conscious
mind works out the plan or solves the problem while, in the
background, our unconscious mind competently performs the
familiar task.

In the second circumstance, however, when both tasks are taxing
or novel, our conscious mind cannot work on them both at the
same time. Multi-tasking does not happen. What our brains can
do is to switch from one task to the other. The cost of this is in
the delays and errors that switching and restarting cause. Let's
see how this works.

How your brain delivers multi-tasking – or not

At the front of your brain – right behind your forehead – is a
bit of your frontal lobe called Brodmann area 10. While nobody

knows its precise function, a lot of evidence now points to area 10 being central to our ability to stop doing something and then come back to it later and pick up where we left off. So it creates the illusion of being able to multi-task because it allows us to chop from one task to another rapidly, and still recall where we were.

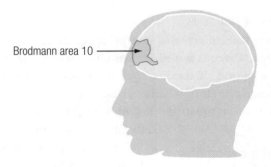

Brodmann area 10

In fact, we are even better at switching tasks than this suggests. Russian psychologist Bluma Zeigarnik noticed that waiters seemed to remember orders only as long as the order was in the process of being served. Once it had been served, they forgot it. Experiments Zeigarnik conducted in 1927 showed that we remember interrupted tasks better than completed ones.

The problems with multi-tasking

One of the most recent studies of multi-tasking was done at Stanford University and compared people who multi-task a lot or a little when using electronic media. The three researchers (Eyal Ophir, Clifford Nass and Anthony Wagner) wanted to find out if the ability to multi-task led to higher performance than the preference to complete one task at a time. Their conclusions were definitive: compared to the low multi-taskers, the researchers found nothing that the high multi-taskers performed better at. In particular, they found three consistent weaknesses, which I shall describe as: being stuck at 'on', disorganised filing, and contamination.

Stuck at 'on'

When faced with multiple images and asked to focus on one type of image, the multi-taskers were less able to ignore irrelevant stimuli. It is as if their minds are stuck at 'on' and they absorb all information available without filtering out the irrelevant data effectively, as the low multi-taskers could.

Disorganised filing

High multi-taskers are also poorer at retaining information in their brains. There is a well-known effect which proves that we all need a period of time to lock information into our short-term memories before it fades away. If we do not get a break in the flow of stimulation, that opportunity is lost to us. One of the dangers of our modern need to be constantly phoning, texting and using hand-held devices is that we may suffer diminished recall of important information – just think of children leaving a classroom and immediately turning on their phones.

> we all need a period of time to lock information into our short-term memories

Contamination

The final weakness of multi-taskers was observed when the groups were introduced to two different tasks, and then asked to complete just one of them. The multi-taskers were far less able to put the other task out of their minds. This contamination effect diminished their performance of the required task.

Do you remember Brodmann area 10? Because this is in a part of our brain that develops late, children are poor at multi-tasking. As we age, this part starts to deteriorate, so older adults are also less skilled at multi-tasking. It is young adults who are best able to screen out unwanted stimuli.

Peak performance

Switching rapidly from one task to another introduces delays and errors that can make multi-tasking far less effective than doing one thing at a time and working through it from start to finish. However, one final factor is of interest to us. If we receive too little stimulation our brain can be impoverished, so a little stimulation, whether it is art on the walls, music in the background, or caffeine in the blood system, can actually increase our performance to a peak.

Making choices to become more effective

Being effective is as much about what you do not do as it is about what you do. The Pareto principle, named after Italian economist Vilfredo Pareto, suggests that we can get 80 per cent of the benefit of our efforts by focusing on the most valuable 20 per cent of the possible activities we could take on. When faced with something that needs to be done, we have five choices we could make:

> being effective is as much about what you do not do as it is about what you do

1. We could get on with it – Do.
2. We could get someone else to do it – Delegate.
3. We could do it later – Delay.
4. We could do a part of it – Diminish.
5. We could leave it – Drop.

The most important 'D' of all, however, is D for decide; we must make a decision, otherwise all we are doing is procrastinating. To minimise your workload, and so make you as effective as possible, we will review the five 'D's' in reverse order, and then finish the section with some advice about how to tell other people if you are going to delay, diminish or drop the task.

Drop it

The Brilliant Question to ask yourself is: 'what if I don't do it?' Think through the consequences, and if there are none, or if the consequences are entirely acceptable to you, then just drop the task entirely. In thinking about the consequences, your first point of reference will be your goals and the outcomes you have set yourself in your OATS planning. If the task does not contribute to these, and if not completing it does not diminish your ability to achieve your goals or outcomes, you must consider dropping it.

Of course, there are some things that we do need to do that contribute to neither, but the penalties for failing to comply mean we cannot drop them – tax returns immediately spring to mind. However, you still have plenty of options.

Diminish it

The Brilliant Question to ask yourself is: 'What if I only do part of it?' How can you make the task smaller? Even in the world of tax returns there are simplified forms and procedures that may be available to you.

In general you are searching for a way to cut down the scope of the task, so you can get it done more quickly and effectively. The bigger and more complex the task, the more likely it is that this approach will be helpful. And if it is really a basket of tasks, which we can call a project, then this becomes a standard part of the project process.

Consider the scope of something as everything that needs to get done. Who decides where the boundaries are? Your job is to challenge the boundaries and try to reduce the scope, to give yourself less to do. And if you cannot reduce the scope, there are still options for some of the components.

Delay it

The Brilliant Question to ask yourself is: 'What if I do it later?' This question is not about procrastination. If the task can be deferred to a later time, or even date, you have more opportunity to schedule it into a convenient time slot. That time may be more convenient because by then you will have better information, more skills or experience, or be working on a related topic and so have all of the preparation already done. The ability to delay a task gives you control over it. Who does their tax return on the day the paperwork comes through the door? Brilliant time managers will schedule it to suit themselves, while making sure it will be complete well in advance of the statutory deadline – unless they have an Octopus personality, in which case they will probably file their return in the last week, if not on the last day!

Delegate it

The Brilliant Question to ask yourself is: 'What if someone else does it?' To use your time most effectively you need to decide what you should do and what you can safely delegate to someone else. In this case we are considering the options of delegating, allocating work, and buying services. Anyone could repair even the most complex fault in their car; most of us, however, would consider the time required to get the training and the cost of buying the necessary equipment to be a good reason to pay a professional mechanic to do the work for them. Likewise, while most tax forms are well within the competence of the people who receive them, some of us choose to pay a tax specialist or accountant to prepare our tax return for us.

Delegation – and the need to do it well – is such an important time-management topic that the whole of Chapter 9 is dedicated to it.

Do it

What if you have asked your four Brilliant Questions and you don't like the answers to any of them? Not doing it is not an option and you have to do all of it. It must be done now, and there is nobody who could do it for you. There is only one option left: just do it!

Even here you may still have a little wiggle room. Unless the task is very quick – no more than four or five minutes, say – it is unwise to do it immediately. Finish what you are working on first, or at least get to a suitable break point, before re-evaluating your priorities.

brilliant tip

Set yourself a rigid time limit for activities such as reading emails, writing a letter, weeding the lawn, or getting your shopping. This will reduce your temptation to get distracted.

Drop, Diminish or Delay – Telling people

If you do decide to delay, diminish, or even drop a task, then somebody may be upset by your decision. Tackle their expectations immediately, because the longer you delay, the harder it will be to tell them and the harder it will be for them to hear. They may have plans to make, so leaving them with an expectation that you will be doing the job now can mislead them and cause them to make plans and arrangements that they will subsequently need to amend.

You may be tempted to break the bad news in stages. Instead of telling me you won't be carrying out the PTA survey for me, you may just tell me that you are busy and will need to put it off. When I next ask you, you put it off a bit longer and also suggest a smaller survey. All the time, you are thinking: 'I need to get out of this hole.' Always break bad news in one go: death by a thousand cuts is more painful and ignites a greater sense of mistrust and betrayal than an honest statement of your true intent. In Chapter 8 you will learn how to say 'no' with confidence and integrity.

More effective meetings

There was a humorous poster doing the rounds in the 1980s and 1990s and it may still be on office noticeboards throughout Britain. It said:

Are you lonely?
Work on your own?
Hate having to make your own decisions?

THEN HOLD A MEETING!

You can get to see other people
Offload decisions and sleep in peace
Feel important and impress colleagues...

AND ALL ON COMPANY TIME!

Meetings: The practical alternative to work

But meetings *are* work. They are where we sell, decide, inform, share, influence, learn, plan, negotiate, make progress and create. What is important is that you make your time at meetings as effective as you possibly can. This means two things: spend less time in meetings and use the time you do spend well.

Spending less time in meetings

You already know all the ways there are to spend less time in meetings: Drop, Diminish, Delay and Delegate. Let's examine each in turn.

Drop

How many meetings do you go to that are really not worth attending at all? There are five types of meeting and one of them serves no purpose at all. Some meetings focus on possibilities: their purpose is to generate ideas. Some focus on opportunities: they evaluate and narrow down the ideas to decide what to do. The third type of meeting is about action: in this we make plans, solve problems, make decisions and allocate responsibilities. The fourth type of meeting is all about building or extending relationships, sharing information, and creating a shared under-standing. The final type of meeting is the type you can drop: these meetings are rituals; we hold them because we have always held them and now no-one remembers why. They serve no purpose, and if you cannot get them stopped, then at least you can stop attending them.

Some meetings of any of the other four types will not be discussing something that you consider to be important enough to you. Always evaluate the need for your attendance at a meeting critically.

Diminish

There are a number of brilliant tactics to make the meetings you do attend shorter. First, you can attend just part of the meeting, either leaving after the parts you are interested in have been covered, or arriving part-way through and skipping irrelevant parts. If you arrange this courteously with the Chair, this will not be seen as rude in most places.

You can also reduce the length of meetings by listening more than you talk. If more people did this, our meetings would be far shorter and more pleasant. Better preparation and reading background material will also reduce the time you spend in the meeting. Some ways to diminish a meeting are only open to the Chair of the meeting, but we can all influence the Chair, for example: to create tighter agendas, more effective circulation of pre-reading, and reducing the meeting's content to only things that require all present to contribute to.

One particular time stealer at a meeting is the 'red herring'. This is a topic that comes up and everyone knows it is not what the meeting has been convened for. Despite this, the meeting gets caught in discussing this. While it is the Chair's job to stop the discussion, it is everyone's responsibility to identify red herrings and alert the Chair to the need to stop.

Finally, when people stand rather than sit, meetings go more quickly. They are slowed down, on the other hand, by tea and biscuits, which give attendees a sense of comfort, relaxation and occasion. Reportedly, the UK government's Cabinet meetings have no tea or coffee available.

Delay

By delaying a meeting you may find that the need for it disappears. Be careful not to create a bigger problem, but some matters will get dealt with by other means, if nobody meets.

Delegate

Do not assume that you are the only person who can attend a particular meeting. Who else could go in your place? You may have a dozen good reasons why nobody else could do it, but ask yourself what would happen if you were away with a long-term illness.

Use your time in meetings well

An effective meeting starts with a Brilliant agenda, which has five sections. This is based on the OATS principle.

1. Title and time

   The title of the meeting should state its purpose, so everyone knows why they are attending.

2. Outcomes

   Next, the agenda should list the outcomes that the meeting organiser wants to achieve by the end of the meeting.

3. Agenda

   The third section sets out the agenda items that the meeting will cover, to deliver the outcomes. Each agenda item should have an indication of the time allocated to it.

4. Key information

   Set out a list of information that you are either circulating with the agenda, or that you expect attendees to refer to in advance. Preparation by each person is key to an effective meeting.

5. Parking Lot

   Leave some blank space at the bottom of your agenda for participants to note items that the Chair defers to a later meeting or discussion afterwards. This allows everyone to see how red herrings and other peripheral issues will be dealt with, without the meeting getting side-tracked.

---

brilliant tip

Been interrupted? Treat it like a meeting and ask:

● What do you want to happen?

● How can I help?

● What do I need to know?

Now you can assess how to deal with the interruption.

Keeping to time

The first secret to keeping to time is starting on time. The best way to break a cultural habit of late arrival is to start the meeting on time with whoever is present, and to refuse to re-open issues that have been discussed and decided in the absence of one or two late arrivals. Good chairing will then keep the meeting on track. This means keeping an eye on everyone and being prepared to stop people when they have made their point, terminate discussions when they are going round and round the same point, and summarising and moving on when the time is right.

After the meeting

A good meeting Chair will also make beneficial use of participants' time by closing the meeting well and following up with effective minutes and a review process. Closing the meeting well requires that all decisions are recorded and reiterated, as are all commitments made by participants, and their deadlines. Thanks and praise for a meeting well conducted will also reinforce good behaviours by participants. After the meeting, send out succinct and accurate minutes, and then follow up to ensure allocated actions are carried out by the agreed deadlines.

Reading more effectively

Guess what: effective reading starts with only reading what matters, so start with the question: 'can I drop, diminish, delay, or delegate this reading?' If you can, you have already taken control. This section will give you some tips on how to read more effectively the articles, books, reports and websites that you choose to read. We will break the reading process down into seven stages: preparation, preview, scanning, alighting, focusing, noting and reviewing. Remember, though, just because you start reading something, you are not committed to finishing it – not even this book!

Preparation

Start by reflecting on why you want to read a book or an article, and also consider what you already know about the topic it discusses. Doing this will allow your brain to find the right mental filing cabinet and open the correct drawer in it. This will help you to store and retain the information you read.

Preview

Now preview the book by looking at the contents. This will serve two purposes: it will help you to decide what depth of reading is merited, and it will also help you to understand the book's structure, pick up its key messages, and figure out where to find what you want in it.

It will also help you retain important information. By understanding the book's structure, not only do you have the right drawer open in your mental filing cabinet, but now you are laying out in your mind the right files, in the right sequence. This step corresponds to the Activities – or Agenda, in this context – step in the OATS principle.

Scanning

Now scan the whole book, report or article to see where important ideas or information catch your eye. This will help you estimate how long you will need to spend, and so corresponds to the Time step in the OATS principle.

Alighting

As you scan the document, alight on the interesting bits and check them out further, by skim-reading them. A handy tip is that you can often get the gist of a section in a book or report by reading the first and last paragraphs and reviewing any tables or figures.

Focusing

When you spot an important section, you need to focus on it and read it properly. Up until now, none of the tips have been about reading faster; they have been about reading only what is of real value to you. Here, we will see three ways you can read paragraphs more quickly and still retain and understand the information within them. These techniques do work, and people who naturally read quickly use one, two or all three of them. We will consider: quieting your inner voice, controlling your eye movements, and the size of the groups of words you look at.

Quieting your inner voice

When you read this sentence, is there a voice in your head speaking these words? This is how a lot of people read, hearing each word as if they were reading out loud. It is called 'sub-vocalising'. The problem with sub-vocalising is that it slows your reading down because the fastest rate you will be able to read at is limited by the rate at which your mind can internally voice the words.

Faster readers do not sub-vocalise. We do not need to hear the words to understand them, so start to practise reading without internally speaking the words on the page.

Controlling your eye movements

Faster readers are also better able to scan their eyes smoothly across a page, following lines of text at a constant rate. Poorer readers, on the other hand, tend to jump about, rest on some parts of a line for longer, and flit back and forth. This will waste time and again does nothing to improve comprehension.

One way to practise smoother eye movements is to follow a pointer. Holding a pencil and scanning it smoothly along each line of text at a constant rate will give your eyes something to follow. As you get better at absorbing the content, without sub-vocalising, you can increase the speed of movement of your pencil tip. Eventually, you will train your eyes and you will be able to dispense with the pencil. Keep it close at hand, though; you'll need it for something else.

The size of the groups of words you look at

The last thing to work on is the blocks of text that your eyes see. Our eyes can take in information from an area of a page that is bigger than one word, so fixing on one word at a time will slow your reading. Instead, scan across the line and fix on two words at a time, then three. The larger the groups of text you fix on, the bigger the chunks of meaning you take in at a time.

You may want to use your trusty pencil to help you with this; it can speed up your moves from one fixation to the next, and guide you to bigger chunks. The most effective readers fix on word clusters of three to five words. This group size matches the structure of language. Let's take an example; a quote from George Bernard Shaw:

'People are always blaming circumstances for what they are. I don't believe in circumstances. The people who get on in this world are the people who get up and look for the circumstances they want, and, if they can't find them, make them.'

Now let's divide this quote into chunks for more effective reading:

'People are always blaming circumstances for what they are. I don't believe in circumstances. The people who get on in this world are the people who get up and look for the circum-stances they want, and, if they can't find them, make them.'

Noting

If you want to understand deeply and retain a large proportion of what you read, then it is worth investing in active reading. Now you are also starting to note down key features. It is the act of noting, rather than the notes themselves, that helps understanding and retention, but the physical notes make it easier to re-find the information quickly at a later date. I said you'd need your pencil again ...

> it is the act of noting, rather than the notes themselves, that helps understanding and retention

Here are five top ways to do this, without keeping a separate notebook. Most of these require you to have the mind-set that books and magazines are for reading and learning from, not for keeping in a pristine state.

1. Underlining key words, phrases and sentences.
2. Using highlighters, rather than underlining.
3. Making notes in the margins.
4. Putting sticky notes on relevant pages and making notes on these.
5. Making notes on the end pages of your book.

If you are reading online, there are a range of software tools to facilitate adding your own notes to public web pages. Examples include Google's Sidewiki, MyStickies, and Wired Marker.

Reviewing

The last step is to review what you have read. Scan back over the whole document and think about how the material compared with your expectations. Did it answer the questions you had and deliver what you wanted? To what extent did it give you new information or confirm what you already knew? What was the most important point you got from it? By taking a few minutes to reflect on your reading, you will lock the essential messages into your memory.

Beware!

Here is a Brilliant quote from Woody Allen: 'I took a speed-reading course and read *War and Peace* in twenty minutes. It involves Russia.' Always treat speed-reading techniques with scepticism. While we can all improve our reading speeds, there is a limit to the speed you can attain and with it retain any useful information, and there will always be trade-offs between speed and retention.

Conquer your stress

Trying to get too much done can lead to the symptoms of stress. And if bad tempers, sleepless nights and recurring colds were not enough, stress also leads to mistakes that exacerbate the feelings of being out of control and not having enough time.

Stress is an inevitable part of life for many of us, and as long as it is not sustained for too long, it is unlikely to do any permanent harm. However, in the short term, the mistakes it causes can be embarrassing, or worse. So we will start by looking at three of the symptoms of stress for time management, and what you can do to manage them, and then we will tackle the bigger question of how you can take control of stress itself.

Three time-management symptoms of stress

Mistakes are often the first signs of stress – particularly if you are someone who prides yourself on getting things right and being reliable. Typical mistakes are: mislaying things, forgetting things, and getting things wrong. Here are some handy hints for each scenario, to help you through the stressful times.

Whoops, I mislaid it

Losing things is an absolutely typical symptom of stress – and losing them far more often. The first thing that stress does is affect the way we process our vision. When we are under stress our vision narrows, so that we focus very tightly on the thing we are looking at and we become less aware of things in our wider field of vision – our peripheral vision. This can lead us to fail to notice something that is literally in front of us. We can look at the mess on our desk, but not spot our mobile phone unless we look straight at it. So when you are looking for something, asking a colleague or friend to look in the obvious places often results in a quick find!

Good habits will also help. If you train yourself to always put your car keys on the hook in the hall, then at times of stress that's where they will be, because, without thinking, that's where you automatically put them when you got home yesterday.

Whoops, I forgot it

When we are stressed, we more easily forget the sort of things we would easily remember at other times. Here are three techniques to ensure you remember that important thing – in addition to your normal systems of diaries, to-do lists and personal organisers.

Technique 1

Make a note and put the note somewhere that you will inevitably discover it. For example, if you want to be sure to phone Aunt Ethel as soon as you get home, wrap a note around your front-door key. If you want to remember to get petrol on the way out of town, put a note on the dashboard of your car.

Technique 2

Send yourself a message. A great way to remind yourself what you need to do at home this evening is to phone home and leave a message on your answerphone, or ask your partner to write a note and put it somewhere you will see it when you get home. Sending yourself emails between your work and your home can also be a great reminder.

Technique 3

Learn to use memory anchors. Create powerful visual images that link things you will see at a certain time with the things you want to remember to do at that time. For example, if I want to remember to email a particular article to Rob when I get into the office tomorrow, I might visualise Rob's head popping out of my computer screen and a hand coming out and grabbing the magazine from my desk drawer. If the image is vivid enough (and making it absurd or salacious will help), then as soon as I see my computer, that image will follow automatically and I will remember to email the article to Rob. Should I worry that I will now always see that image when I get to my desk? No. Remember the Zeigarnik effect, which we saw earlier in this chapter? Once the task is completed, Brodmann's area 10 will drop it out of my memory.

Whoops, I got it wrong

Error rates go up when we are stressed, so it is important to implement good procedures to systematically reduce the opportunity for error. As tailors say, 'measure twice: cut once'.

Getting things right first time means disciplining yourself to check and check again. For example, on letters and written reports, be scrupulous in looking for data errors, spelling mistakes, faulty analysis, grammatical slips, mis-quotes and wrong attributions, sloppy definitions and, perhaps worst of all, getting a name wrong.

Take control of your stress

Taking control of stress means one thing: taking back control. We feel stressed when we feel that we do not have control over an important aspect of our lives. This subject could fill a whole book, but, simply, there are four areas where we can regain control: our thoughts,

taking control of stress means one thing: taking back control our physiology, our environment and our attitudes. We will look briefly at each.

Take control of your thoughts

At times of stress, our thoughts betray us by seeing things at their bleakest. It is important to seize control of that little voice in your head that will tell you how bad things are, how useless you are, and how inevitable failure is. Instead, use it to focus on what you can control, the resources that are available to you and the successes you are having. There is always something positive or some small victory to hold onto, so notice this and reinforce its significance.

Take control of your physiology

When we feel stressed, our breathing becomes shallow, our bodies become hunched and tense, our eating suffers and our sleep patterns deteriorate. Force yourself to take slow, deep breaths to relax yourself. Make time for exercise – even if it is just walking – to give your body back its natural posture. Choose to eat healthy foods and take your time over eating them, to put proper nutrients back into your body. In particular, ensure you drink enough water, because dehydration will compromise your mind's ability to think clearly and keep a proper perspective on events. And prioritise relaxation and sleep.

One of the most powerful aspects of your physiology is using the twelve facial muscles it takes to smile. When we activate these, signals go back to our brain that release hormones which make us feel an increased sense of well-being. It is not simply that feeling happy will make you smile; smiling will make you feel happy. So make time for fun and laughter.

Take control of your environment

Making small changes to your physical environment – even if it is just tidying up your work space – can restore an important feeling of control. If you can, carve out a part of your home where you can rearrange things to be just as you like them. Use colour, art, ornaments, scents and music to create the mood you want, rather than the one you have.

Take control of your attitudes

A lot of stress comes from adopting the attitudes we think we ought to have, rather than the ones that really suit us. For example, feeling we have to rush and be busy all the time can leave some of us constantly exhausted. Instead, devise an attitude of finding smarter ways to get more done in less time. Some people have an attitude that failure is a sign of weakness, but if you can acknowledge failure as a necessary part of life, and even as a sign of the strength to try new things, then you will transform your response to setbacks. Another example is the need to be strong for the people around you. When you acknowledge that other people want to help you as much as you want to help them, and that a willingness to ask for help *is* a sign of strength, then you will feel a burden lift from your shoulders.

 **recap**

- An extreme Elephant personality means that you can get too engrossed in something, lose track of time, and fail to do all of the things you need to.

- An extreme Octopus mentality means you can try to do too much at once, and fail to finish everything to a sufficient standard.

- Multi-tasking is not as effective as focusing on a single thing then moving on.

- Faced with a new task, don't do it without first considering whether you can delegate, delay, diminish, or even drop it.

- Make your meeting time more effective by spending less time at meetings and using the time you are there well.

- Follow a seven-step reading process to spend less time reading and be able to retain more information.

CHAPTER 6

Focus on priorities to take control of your time

I n Chapter 2, you saw how to monitor the way in which you use your time. When you survey an unproductive day or, worse, an unproductive week, it will often seem as if some thief has stepped in and stolen your time. This chapter is about how that happens and what you can do about it.

When you analyse where your lost time is going, you will find two ways in which your time gets stolen from you:

1. Some of us lose most of our time because we fritter it away doing nothing very much. This is easier than doing something important, which takes concentration and involves the possibility of failure. So, rather like a hedgehog, it is, perhaps, easier to curl up into a little ball of inaction; it feels safe. Of course, most of us feel uncomfortable with total inaction, so we replace meaningful activity with meaningless 'displacement' activities. This is procrastination; putting off what we know we need to do.

2. Other people lose most of their time by doing too much. They react to everything that crops up as if it is vitally important and are consequently forever busy. They go for this and they go for that, without discrimination. I call these people 'Gophers'.

The four sections in this chapter deal with the problems that Hedgehogs and Gophers face. First, we'll look at the Hedgehog's problem of procrastination, and then at the Gopher's problem of eternal busy-ness. Then we will review one of the most powerful tools for time management, the distinction between what is important and what is merely urgent. Finally, we will close the chapter with a review of the four greatest time thieves of all, and how you can handle them.

The Hedgehog: procrastination

The Hedgehog's response to a perceived threat is to curl up into a small ball until it goes away. We do that sometimes, too, and the result is putting off important tasks that we know we should be tackling now. The first step to conquering this behaviour is to understand why it happens, and then to consider how to tackle it.

Why we procrastinate

The fundamental reason for procrastination is a sense of being overwhelmed. The task before us seems like a huge mountain. Often, the benefit of doing what needs to be done is far greater than the effort of tackling the task but, like a little mountain in the foreground obscuring the far greater peak behind it, we don't see the pay-off as clearly as the work required to achieve it.

> the fundamental reason for procrastination is a sense of being overwhelmed

The bigger our foreground task gets, the worse the problem is. When we have two or three magazines to read, or a couple of centimetres of papers to sort through, or the lawn has got too long, or yesterday's dishes are all in a pile, the job is daunting. But if we leave things, then there will be five or six magazines, seven or eight centimetres of papers, nine or ten centimetre-long grass, or two days' dishes. Now the task is becoming an epic one.

'**... and I'm feeling pretty cosy, curled up in my little ball.**' Doing nothing won't challenge my sense of well-being, while taking on this job will be uncomfortable.

'**... and what if it all goes wrong?**' What if I fail, and then get blamed for it? There may be consequences to failure, which I can avoid by not doing anything.

'**... and what I'm doing now really is important.**' It always is! Somehow, we can manage to persuade ourselves that the most trivial things are vital to us, when the alternative is doing something we'd really rather not do.

'**... and anyway, I've got loads of time.**' Some of us work best to a deadline, but kidding yourself about how far away that deadline is and the amount of time you need to meet it is a way of setting yourself up to fail.

'**... and I'm going to fail anyway.**' Here's the killer reason for procrastination, which becomes a self-fulfilling prophecy. It feels better to prove yourself right in your fatalism than to succeed at what you want to do.

Getting over the blocks

We have all been there with those excuses, but as Robert Herrick says in the opening line of his poem: 'Gather ye rosebuds while ye may'. Here are twelve ways to uncurl your inner hedgehog and overcome procrastination.

Create a sense of discomfort

If procrastination involves a feeling of comfort with how things are, then you can beat it by feeling uncomfortable with the situation. If you don't do it, what will happen – or not happen – which will cause you a problem? Focus on this, and then amplify this effect by getting a sense that this problem could arise sooner than you think.

Focus on the future

This combines nicely with the previous technique: think about how great you will feel when the job is done. Mowing the lawn may be an unpleasant chore to you, but think about how great it will be to sit down afterwards with a beer. Washing the dishes may not be fun, but having a clean, tidy kitchen will be fabulous.

Baby steps

The next technique is to create momentum. Once you get started with things, they often seem easy; it's just the problem of getting started. So don't set out to tackle that whole pile of papers; just take one from the pile and set out to deal with that. Once you have made a start, you are on your way.

I know, don't set out to clean the dishes, just empty the sink and fill it with hot water. Okay, maybe then you might clean a couple of glasses, and then, before you know it, the job is done.

Worst things first

There's an old saying that if the first thing you do in the morning is to eat a live frog, then you will know that you won't have to do anything worse for the rest of the day. So grit your teeth and get your worst job of the day out of the way, first thing. There is even a book called *Eat That Frog!*

Least things first

If you really aren't feeling in the mood, then perhaps you should just not do anything? No. Do something, but pick the smallest, easiest thing on your today list to get you back into the mood of being productive. The success you have in doing that will motivate you to do the next thing. If there is nothing sufficiently small on your today list, look for a small job on your to-do list. Or, failing that, set yourself a simple task like reading an article in a magazine or tidying your desk or workplace. But make sure it is a clearly bounded task; the worst thing a Hedgehog can do is take on a low-value, but long-lasting, job.

Walk to work

Many people who work from home struggle to get started in the morning. One great way to get started is to walk to work. Rather than just get up, get washed, get breakfast and then expect to get going, when you are ready, take yourself for a ten- to twenty-minute walk. This will clear your head and make the transition from 'home life' to 'work life' much clearer. The combination of fresh air, exercise and sunlight is one of the most motivating cocktails you can take, and, if it helps, stop somewhere for a coffee or tea on your way.

Also, if you often don't feel like working, resist the temptation to dress down when you work at home; instead, dress for work. For many of us, the way we are dressed has a profound influence on how we feel – when we dress casually, we feel casual. Dressing for work reminds you that today is a day to focus on getting your work done.

Short sprints, rather than long distance running

Taking on a big task can be made easier by working in short bursts of high concentration, rather than one long slog. We all have a natural period of time within which we work well, and then our energy starts to drop quite quickly. This varies from around fifteen minutes up towards an hour, although, for most people, it is between twenty and thirty minutes. You may already know your concentration span and, if so, work to a convenient point near to the limit of your peak concentration, and then take a break.

If you don't know how long your peak attention periods last, experiment. Try working in fifteen-minute bursts, then twenty minutes, and onwards until you find out when you start to get fatigued. This will tell you your optimum task length.

Celebrate each success

Perhaps the greatest motivator of all is success, so make a point of acknowledging and celebrating each success. For the

make a point of acknowledging and celebrating each success

smallest triumphs, a mental pat on the back and acknowledgement of 'that went well', or 'I'm pleased with that' will be enough. For bigger victories, reward yourself with a break, a biscuit, or something else nice. As your successes get bigger, then step up the scale of your celebrations. Whenever you celebrate your success, you feel good about yourself, which makes you feel more confident, which leads to better performance and therefore better results, and thus to more success. Which means you can celebrate more. It's a virtuous cycle.

Slice up your elephant

You cannot eat an elephant whole; but if you slice it thinly enough and spread the meal over enough sittings then you can finish it. Bite-sized portions of work are less intimidating, so split up your project into small tasks, and make each one short and simple enough to do in one sitting – matched to your optimum task length.

By breaking your project into multiple small tasks, you will also have multiple successes in completing portions of the work, giving you the opportunity for multiple celebrations.

Choose your moment

Another factor that can have an impact on how easy you find it to get started is when you choose to start: a substantial task needs substantial energy, so starting it at the end of the day or in one of your low moments will not help. On the other hand, if it is a small, but unpleasant-seeming task, like washing out that disgusting mug that got left behind the sofa, then doing it when you are a little tired would be the right time to get it out of the way, and free you to do more substantial work when you are feeling more fresh.

Focus

Preventing the feeling of procrastination is an essential skill. By focusing on what is important, you are less likely to want to put off tasks. By using a today list to hone your to-do list down to what is important now, and by using your to-don't list to get rid of things that you aren't going to do anyway, you will turn an endless list of tasks into a very manageable workload. You will learn all about today lists and to-don't lists in Chapter 10.

Create a commitment

If 'Write the monthly key data report' is on my today list, I would like to think I'll do it – even if it is not my favourite job. But if I want to give myself that extra push, why don't I tell people it is due out at 9 o'clock tomorrow morning. Now I have made a conspicuous commitment that I'll have it done today, so I will activate Jiminy Cricket – the little voice of my conscience – who will remind me and put pressure on me to get it done. The more push I want, the more people I will tell and I will also tell the more important people in my circle. Most of us work to a deadline, and many of us need there to be an external driver for that deadline. If I don't have one, I can create it.

The Gopher: always going for it

Whenever they get an opportunity – of any sort – Gophers will just 'go for it'. This gives Gophers an awesome ability to get things done and, because they always step up and volunteer, it also makes them very popular people to have around a workplace or in a social club. Everyone wants to have a Gopher around them.

However, the result is that Gophers are always rushing around, without any strategic planning about what is the right thing to do, and how to do it efficiently. They can also find themselves over-committing their time and, consequently, they can either let people down or, more often, sacrifice their own legitimate outcomes in favour of those of other people. Gophers start out buoyant and enthusiastic about everything, but they can end up seriously stressed.

The challenge for a Gopher is knowing *when* to go for it.

When to go for it

If you are something of a Gopher, then here is a process to help you evaluate each opportunity; it is called SCOPE the task.

Stop   Before you rush in and go for it without thinking, just stop.

Clarify   Ask questions, find out all you can about the task.

Options   What are your options? Which is the best?

Proceed   Follow through on your best option.

Evaluate   When you are finished, evaluate the decision you made.

This process provides you with a great way to make decisions and, if you evaluate the outcome when the job is done, a learning process by which you can hone your strategic instincts. When something urgent comes up, you can improve the quality of your response by writing it down. The act of writing forces you to stop, and then activates the rational parts of your brain and makes it assess the priority objectively.

⚡ brilliant questions

When you SCOPE the task, here are four Brilliant Questions to ask yourself to help understand your options:

1. What will happen if you do it?

2. What will happen if you don't do it?

3. What will not happen if you do it?

4. What will not happen if you don't do it?

Establishing boundaries

Breaking out of the cycle of 'always going for it' is also a matter of establishing the right boundaries, and knowing what you won't do, as well as what you will.

brilliant exercise

When you create a to-don't list of all the things on your to-do list that you can drop, you will have less to worry about. Make a new to-don't list for next week. On it, list all of your Gopher habits that you would like to drop. For example:

To-don't

- Pick up the phone when I am in the middle of an important piece of work that requires my concentration
- Open my email software until I have planned my day and done the first thing
- Open my post as soon as it arrives
- Look at my favourite book website unless I have a specific book to order
- Get chatting with someone when I get my tea or coffee.

Brilliant choices are not about how busy or relaxed you are: they are about how you respond to the things that you don't truly have the time to do. Do you view them as choices not made, which make way for other, more pressing, priorities; or are they lost opportunities that represent frustration and disappointment? When you can take the first of these attitudes, you will conquer your inner gopher. The next section looks at how to do this.

Distinguishing the urgent from the important

President Dwight D. Eisenhower said: 'Most things which are urgent are not important, and most things which are important are not urgent.' Having set your goals (Chapter 4), you will know what things are important, because these are things that contribute in some way to your ability to achieve your goals. Urgent things are merely time critical, but not necessarily important – although they can be.

The four quadrants

There are four possible combinations.

Not Urgent and Important	Urgent and Important
Not Urgent and Not Important	Urgent and Not Important

Urgent and Important tasks

These are tasks that grab your attention and demand action, because they are time critical, and because failing to attend to them has significant consequences. They therefore account for most of our feelings of being out of control. Examples are scheduled activities that are nearing a deadline or customer demands in a business environment. Many people believe that this is where they should focus their energy, but it is a highly reactive zone that does not achieve management of your time; the best it can aspire to is keeping up. With Urgent and Important tasks, you have no choice: you must just get on and do them.

Urgent but not Important tasks

Ring-ring! Most of the calls we receive – by phone or email – are not about urgent matters, nor important ones. But the medium can make them urgent. In the next section of this chapter we will look at how to deal with these time thieves. A lot of meetings come into this category – there would be no great consequence if you were to skip the meeting, yet the fact that it is scheduled gives it an urgency. Urgent and *not* Important things are often important to someone else, so you need to SCOPE the task and decide whether the activity, or the relationship, is important enough to you. If the task really is important to the person who originates it, but not to you, can you delegate it to someone else?

Not Urgent and not Important tasks

These are your time-wasting tasks and displacement activities. The more you can do to eliminate these from your day, the better off you will be. The best thing to do with these is to simply drop them.

But we need to acknowledge how seductive they can be. Have you ever spent good money – up to £2 – on a weekend newspaper and, when you get it home, shaken it out and idly picked up the advertising catalogue that was packaged in with the supplements? You then start to read the one part of the paper you didn't pay for – and you probably knew before you even opened it that you would not be buying anything from it. It's not important and it's not urgent either. If you don't read it now, it will still be on the kitchen table or under the settee a week later.

Not Urgent and *not* Important tasks rob you of valuable time, so only waste your time when you have spare time to waste.

Not Urgent and Important tasks

These are the tasks that give you control over your time. Things that are not urgent now will become so later, so by tackling them early you remove the stress element and give yourself the time to do them well. These are the activities that you can defer and schedule to a time that suits you.

Not Urgent and Important tasks are investments in your goals. They include planning and preparation, rest, relaxation and relationship building. None of these is urgent and you could probably skip that relaxing family meal if you were under pressure. But if you do that too often, then relationships will start to suffer. Deferring your trip to the gym may not make a difference today, but missing it frequently will harm your physical and maybe your emotional well-being.

So focus your quality time onto Important and not Urgent tasks. They will allow you to make real progress towards your goals, and leave you feeling more fulfilled as well as more relaxed, and certainly more productive as well as able to do your work to a higher standard.

Using the model

A great way to use the model is to draw the four boxes on a large sheet of paper or a whiteboard. If you have neither of those, four panels in a door or four areas on a wall will do. Put all of the things facing you this week onto sticky notes and then look at each one in turn. Be ruthless in deciding on the urgency and importance of each one. Ask yourself:

- Is this truly urgent?

  If it is, then it will be something that needs to be dealt with this week, and if it is not, then will it no longer be relevant at the end of the week?

- Is this truly important?

  If it is, then there will be serious consequences if it does not get done or, if it is done, it will move you towards achieving one of your goals.

This is a powerful way to understand your to-do list, and to help you move tasks onto your today or to-don't list.

Dealing with time thieves

Interruptions of all kinds come mostly from the people you work with: your boss, your staff, your colleagues, your suppliers and your customers. They can come in face-to-face interruptions, over the phone, or by email. At home, they come from family members, relatives calling you, friends dropping by, cold calls, and knocks at the door. We will tackle these one at a time.

Face-to-face interruptions

As with any new task, the first thing to do is to SCOPE the interruption:

Stop   Before you deal with it without thinking, just stop.

Clarify   Ask questions, find out what the person wants.

Options	What are your options? Which is the best?
Proceed	Follow through on your best option.
Evaluate	When you are finished, evaluate the decision you made.

A wise former boss of mine, George, gave me some good advice when I first started managing a large team. I was getting frustrated by their constant interruptions; all they wanted was help, advice and support so they could make progress in their own work. George suggested I think about my job as a manager and ask myself what is more important: my work or helping them to do theirs. For some of us, at some times, dealing with interruptions *is our job*.

When you SCOPE your response, there are five options available to you:

1. Respond and act on the interruption.

2. Respond and defer the action, by setting a time.

3. Delegate the response to someone else.

4. Respond and file the information.

5. Reject the interruption – this requires assertiveness and the ability to say 'no' in a positive manner. This is an important skill, so the whole of Chapter 8 is given over to saying 'no'.

brilliant tip

If you do get interrupted, stand up. This makes it unlikely that the other person will sit down, make themselves comfortable and settle in for a long chat. Standing signals readiness to move, and will give the clear impression that you do not have unlimited time.

Controlling interruptions

Randomness is what allows time stealing; you cannot manage what you do not control. So take control by creating time slots in your day when you encourage interruptions, which gives you the opportunity to also set aside time when interruptions are not okay. If you have an 'open door' policy, then a closed door should signal to your colleagues that you do not want interruptions except in emergencies.

> randomness is what allows time stealing; you cannot manage what you do not control

If you work in an open-plan office, this is more difficult. One way is to signal your openness to interruptions with a sign. A small sign saying 'it's okay to interrupt me' invites interruptions when you are working on low-grade tasks. If colleagues get to know this sign, they will also come to notice times when the sign is laid down.

One favourite technique is to book a meeting room and go there to work quietly. This has two advantages. First, by putting a meeting in your diary you will protect time for important work, and second, with a meeting in your diary (or just being gone from your desk) colleagues will not come and interrupt you. If meeting rooms are not available where you work, a local café can be a fair alternative, with better teas and coffees, usually.

Interruptions from your boss

Bosses can be a particular challenge, because of the power imbalance. If they make unreasonable demands on you, enlist their help in prioritising your workload, so that they understand the situation they are putting you in. If their request is reasonable, but challenging, offer them options or suggest a deadline that gives them what they need (which may not be quite what they want) and can show how you are managing your time and responsibilities.

 tip

One of the biggest interruptions is a meeting you don't need to go to. Start to decline invitations to meetings you don't need to attend.

Phones

Mobile phones can give anyone in the world permission to grab your attention and steal your time whenever *they* want it. There is a button on your phone that can help enormously. It turns your phone off. Make sure you have a clear voicemail message that conveys the impression that you want to convey (professional, friendly, efficient), and check your messages frequently. Voicemail allows you to regain control over mobile phone calls.

When you do take a call, whether on a mobile or fixed line, there are some tips to minimise the disruption. We'll look at these before turning to how to make calls efficiently.

Taking calls

When you receive a call, get a notepad or open your daybook, grab a pen, and answer in this order:

1. Greeting first: 'hello, good afternoon'.
2. Introduce yourself with your name and, if appropriate, your position.
3. Ask who you are speaking with and whom they represent.
4. Record this information in your notepad or daybook.
5. Use their name from time to time during the call.

Standing up or sitting with a confident, upright posture not only makes you sound more authoritative, it also conveys a slightly less relaxed tone to your voice. The caller will sense that a long, cosy chat is not quite as welcome as it would be if you were sitting down in a relaxed posture.

If you really want to put some time pressure on the caller, announce how much time you have available at the start of the call: 'Chris, it's great to hear from you. I have about five minutes before I need to prepare for a meeting.' You can even make a virtue of the time pressure and make the caller feel valued: 'Chris, it's great to hear from you. I would love to talk at length with you. Unfortunately I cannot give you the time I want to, right now. Can I call you back at 3pm, so we can speak properly, or is it something we can deal with very quickly?' This gives you back control. If the call needs a very short conversation then you have already been interrupted, so deal with it immediately. If not, you have claimed the right to schedule the conversation to suit you, while indicating that the relationship is more valuable to you than a rushed call.

If you need to cut short a phone conversation, it is better to interrupt yourself than the other person: 'so, to recap ... actually, I've just noticed the time; can I send you a quick summary by email?' Alternatively, signal the end of the conversation, with something like: 'one last thing before I have to go'.

Making calls

The secret to making calls efficiently is to be highly organised about it. Create a contact management system for yourself that tracks who you need to call, and brings the names forward on the right day. The simplest approach is to have a calendar or diary in which you record the calls you need to make against the appropriate week.

A weekly call sheet is usually better than a daily one for scheduled outgoing calls. It gives you the flexibility to plan blocks of calls into convenient slots in your week. If you receive a lot of incoming calls that you put through to voicemail, an answerphone, or an assistant, then you will need a daily call sheet. Whichever approach you take, group your calls to make the process more efficient. Your call sheet creates a closed list that makes completion of the task possible. So create your call sheet based on the today principle, rather than the to-do principle. If you dislike making calls, allocate them into fixed time slots and take a break when you have completed each time allocation.

Before you make your calls, get yourself prepared. Make sure you have scanned relevant papers and have key information ready at hand. Use a daybook to make notes of every call you make or receive. Number each page and then put the date down at the start of your first call of each day. When you make or receive the call, start by recording the name of the person who has called you or the person you are trying to call, and their organisation. You may also want to record the time. Then make key notes on your conversation. If you don't get through, you may want to record what happened. Abbreviations can speed this up:

- NA   No answer
- VM   Voicemail
- VM-NM   Voicemail – no message left
- VM-ML   Voicemail – message left
- MLWC   Message left with colleague

Not getting through to the person you are after can be one of the biggest time stealers when you are making calls. If you speak to a person and they ask you to hold, enquire as to how long a wait you can expect, and consider offering to call back. On the other hand, if you end up in the first circle of hell, otherwise known as an automated call-waiting system, here are three ways to better use your time: try calling back at a less busy time; put the call on a loudspeaker and do something else while you wait; or transfer the call to a cordless phone, ideally with a headset, so you can leave your desk entirely and make yourself a cup of tea, or take the opportunity to travel the world.

 **tip**

> Waiting time need not be wasted time – clear a few emails or tidy
> your kitchen, desk, hallway while you are on hold.
>
> If you have to wait in a real queue – for example, at a Post Office –
> take a magazine to read.

One particular example is deliberate screening of calls by secre-
taries. This is their job, so confrontation will not help: your best
tactic is to make an ally of them. It's not urgent, but it is important to invest time in building a relationship with the secretary
who has the power to put you through or not. However, if you
want to bypass a secretary, then most keep fairly standard hours:
9–5. To save time, call their boss before 9am or after 5:30pm and
you may get through directly.

Finally, be ready to leave (or not) an answerphone or voicemail
message. The alternative is to be unprepared and then hang
up and have to waste time calling again so that you can leave
a thought-out message. When you speak to a machine, speak
slowly and always repeat your name and any phone number you
leave, at the end of the message.

Email

Email can be a constant distraction when you are using your
computer, so do turn the software off and, unless they are part
of your organisation's formal operational process, disable the
alerts which break into your thought patterns whenever they
like.

Before you use email for any message, always ask: Is email the
right tool for the job?

Dealing with incoming email

The best way to deal with incoming email is in fixed time slots after you have completed a significant task. First, scan the headers and delete anything that is neither urgent nor important. Then handle the rest by dealing with each item, either:

- Review and don't respond – then file or delete.
- Review and forward for someone else to respond.
- Respond then file.
- Respond then delete.
- Schedule a full response.

A good way to handle a backlog is to use your email program's sorting function to sort by either sender or conversation thread. This is a good way to batch up emails that go together and reduce your reading time. It also makes filing quicker.

To speed up responding to email, set yourself the objective of replying to any email in a maximum of two sentences. You may not always be able to do this, but you will surprise yourself when you really focus on this.

Sending out email

When you send an email you can pre-empt a lot of wasted time later, by reviewing what you have written to ensure that it is clear and concise, and that any action you require is clearly set out. Make sure that your contact details are all in the message and, above all, read it before sending it to avoid time-stealing misunderstandings. Before you send it, add courtesy words like please and thank you.

Be very careful about how much of other people's time you steal with the indiscriminate use of CC or BCC. Ask yourself: 'will each of these people value the message enough to make the time it takes them to read it seem like a worthwhile use of their precious time?' If the answer is no, don't copy them in.

Finally, consider the timing of your email. If the person you send it to is a brilliant time manager, then even if they are at their computer you cannot expect they will read it as soon as you send it. There can be delays in transmission and in receipt, so if your message really is urgent, call them.

Efficient use of your email system
Modern email systems offer huge numbers of tools to help you use them in a way that suits you. Invest time in learning what options are available to sort and file your information. Certainly create a 'junk folder' and tag 'junk messages' as such so that they can automatically be routed there and avoid stealing your time. Scan then delete the contents of your junk folder every couple of days – in case there is something of value that has been mis-directed.

The worst thief of all

… is you. Ultimately, it is you who steals most of your time, and you are complicit in every theft. When you make the 'easy' choice, or make no choice at all, it may feel as if you are saving time, but if you do not protect the time you have for the things you want to do, you will end up doing things that are important to anyone else but you. Think of the 86,400 seconds in each day as a budget. If someone gave you £86,400 at midnight, and told you would lose every penny that you did not spend wisely over the next 24 hours, you would work hard to find worthwhile things to spend that money on. Why would you do less with an even more precious resource?

> ultimately, it is you who steals most of your time

 recap

- There are twelve ways to overcome procrastination: try one of them now. Now.

- Don't do things just because they are there to do – SCOPE the task first: Stop, Clarify, Options, Proceed, Evaluate.

- Distinguish the important things from the merely urgent and put your focus onto them. When you work on the things that are important but not urgent, you will be in control of your time.

- Control your interruptions; or they will control you.

CHAPTER 7

When to keep going and when to let go

Getting the most done that you possibly can is about persevering – with the right things – and therefore, dropping other things. In this chapter, we shall see how a focus on the right thing feels good, how it returns better results, and how special times can enhance your ability to focus and get more done.

In the first section of this chapter, you will learn about 'flow' – a state of optimum concentration and happiness in which getting things done seems to be effortless and enjoyable. In the second section, we will consider why it is important to focus if you want to excel at anything, and we will examine how to evaluate your time investments objectively. Finally, we will close the chapter with a section about how you can use special times to get more done, and we will identify five different times when you can wring the most out of your day.

Flow

Have you ever got so engrossed in something that when you next look up, a whole hour – or more – has just gone? You weren't aware of passing time at all. I find this often happens when I am writing – just now for instance. This phenomenon has been called 'flow' by American psychologist Mihaly Csikszentmihalyi. In flow, long periods of time seem to pass in an instant.

Comfort zones

Some things are easy to do and when doing them we feel comfortable, if a little bored. In this 'comfort zone', activities are, at their best, relaxing diversions that require some concentration, but little effort. At their worst, they are so trivial that we turn off our minds and go beyond boredom. We don't care, and consequently, we become complacent. Here, mistakes and accidents can happen.

Some other things are beyond our skill level. When the skill gap is at its greatest, we can find ourselves anxious and even panicked by the fear of failure and its consequences. So as result we fail to capitalise on the challenge and learn from it. A moderate level of challenge, just beyond your skill level, is where your senses are at their sharpest and you learn the most.

But what happens when we tackle a task that is highly challenging, and for which we need and have a high level of expertise? These tasks satisfy the first of three conditions for a state of mind known as 'flow'.

What is flow?

Flow is a state in which our sense of time becomes distorted and we become completely absorbed in the activity at hand. Consequently, we lose awareness of the concerns and frustrations of our day-to-day life, and of our physical needs. Time seems to pass without us feeling hungry and we may only later, at the end of the activity, notice how uncomfortably hot or cold we feel. When we are in this flow state, what we are doing becomes an objective in itself, and doing it well for its own sake becomes our primary challenge.

Flow can be hugely beneficial, as it allows us to concentrate for long periods at a time without a break, to do a fabulous job, and to enjoy it at the same time. Indeed, Mihaly Csikszentmihalyi, who coined the term 'flow', described it as the state of optimum experience. The conditions for flow are also the conditions for happiness.

It is also possible to become addicted to flow and to shut yourself off from the real world of cares and frustrations, but for most of us, more flow experiences in our lives will have an enriching effect. While we mostly experience flow during leisure and hobby activities, it is possible to access flow states in all aspects of our lives; from childcare to maintenance, to construction, to paperwork and report-writing.

Creating flow

In his book, *Flow, The Psychology of Happiness*, Csikszentmihalyi says:

 'In theory, any job could be changed so as to make it more enjoyable by following the prescriptions of the flow model.'

He then adds:

'... if workers really enjoyed their jobs they would not only benefit personally, but sooner or later they would almost certainly produce more efficiently and reach all the other goals that now take precedence.'

So, how can you create a flow experience from the things you want to get done? There are three conditions that a flow state requires.

Condition 1: balance skills and challenge

We started this section by looking at how too little challenge leads to boredom and complacency, while too much leads to anxiety and fear. When, however, you are working on something which is highly challenging, but for which you feel you have the right skills, so that you are working at the limit of your capabilities and are being stretched to use them to their fullest extent, this is rewarding. A precise balance of the perceived amount of challenge with your perceived skill level is the first condition for flow. You may have very high levels of skill and be working on something to the most demanding standards, and so feel a huge sense of satisfaction. Note that I can feel the same level of satisfaction from working on a far less challenging task, because I do not share your skill level. You would find my task dull: I would find yours intimidating or even scary.

Condition 2: clear goals

Activities that lead to flow are ones where we feel an intrinsic value in doing them for their own sake – Csikszentmihalyi refers to these by the Greek work 'autotelic', which literally means 'self goal'. To create a flow activity, you must set clear goals for the task. These must be attainable for you

> to create a flow activity, you must set clear goals for the task

and match your skill set and abilities, but not be too easy. Flow activities are also constrained by boundaries, expectations or rules. These can be externally imposed, or ones that you set for yourself.

Condition 3: immediate feedback
The final condition for flow is that the activity must have direct and immediate feedback, so that outcomes (whether successes or failures) are readily apparent to you, and so you can adjust what you are doing to optimise your performance. It is this constant monitoring and review cycle that keeps you locked into your flow state and helps you to drive your performance levels upwards.

brilliant example

The power of goals and feedback has been demonstrated in an experiment by two psychologists, Albert Bandura and Daniel Cervone. In the early 1980s, they measured the performance of eighty student cyclists on a cycling ergo meter and then split them into four groups, which they balanced for gender and ability:

Group A were set goals for performance improvement.

Group B were given no goals, but feedback on their performance.

Group C got both performance goals and feedback.

Group D were a control group and got neither goals nor feedback.

At the end of a training period, the researchers found that the cyclists who had received both clear performance goals and feedback (Group C) had improved their performance by twice as much as any other group. Not surprisingly, the control group (Group D) improved least but, surprisingly, their improvement was only marginally less (21 per cent) than Group A (25 per cent) and Group B (25 per cent).

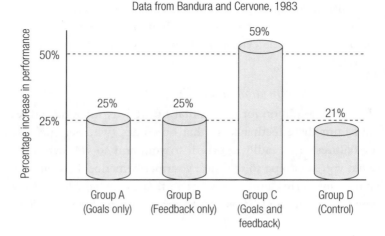

Data from Bandura and Cervone, 1983

Autotelic personalities

Csikszentmihalyi suggested that some people are better able to do things for their own sake, and therefore find it easier to get into flow states than other people. He found that people with 'autotelic personalities' tend to be curious, persistent, interested in all that life has to offer and less self-centred than most of us.

At the other extreme, some people are greatly sensitive to external stimuli and find it hard to get into flow states, or to stay long in them. High multi-taskers may fall into this category, and at the far extreme are attention disorders and schizophrenia, which includes an inability to experience true pleasure, and over-sensitivity to stimuli.

Investing your time

Kenny Rogers won a Grammy Award for his performance of Don Schlitz's song, 'The Gambler'. It became a big hit, and its advice is true in many situations in life: 'You got to know when to hold 'em, know when to fold 'em; know when to walk away, know when to run.'

Poker players know that every hand is a potential winner if it's played right, but to boost your overall odds, you need to choose the right hand to play. So it is with the things you do in life. In this section, we will look first at why you need to choose, and then we will look at how to evaluate your opportunities.

Why you need to choose

The expression 'the learning curve' refers to the rate of improvement in our abilities as we practise a particular skill or craft. A 'steep learning curve' requires that we quickly achieve a high level of competence. But have you noticed that in most of the things you do, your learning curve seems to flatten out? After a certain time, more effort seems not to bring about more improvement. What happens next is crucial.

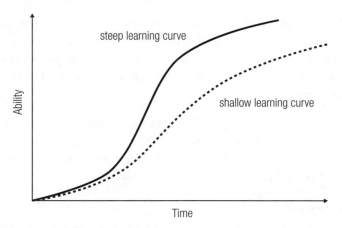

The dip

In his book of the same name, Seth Godin coined the term 'the dip' for the tendency for the learning curve to turn down, so that we seem almost to be going backwards in our learning. More knowledge and experience seems, if anything, to be hampering our performance. This is a stage when our brain is processing our learning and we are starting to analyse what we are doing. This conscious analysis starts to interfere with our ability to exercise the level of skill we have acquired.

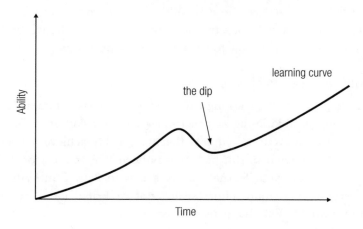

However, the dip is dispiriting. It is easy to lose motivation and give up, because working our way out of the dip takes time and effort. If we do so, though, the reward will be that our learning curve will eventually turn upwards again and we will be on the road to mastery.

Any activity that is worthwhile will have a dip; whether it is a sport, a profession, an art or a hobby. Even many of the things we take for granted, like learning to drive, to cycle and even to walk, have a dip.

The cul-de-sac

With some things, once you get to a level of competence, your learning curve flattens off and no amount of additional practice or study will ever make you any better at doing them. They are easy to master and impossible to excel at. Seth Godin described this type of activity as a cul-de-sac. It is a dead end.

Mundane activities such as sweeping and filing are like this, and so are the fundamentals of professional skills, such as book-keeping. When you master this, there is nothing more to learn:

you can either do it right, or not. So, to excel, you need to add further aspects to your work, like teaching the skill, or interpreting the data.

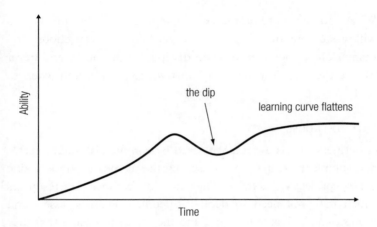

The choice

It is obvious that investing your time in a cul-de-sac activity is of limited value. You might 'have' to do it, but invest no more time and effort than it takes to deliver competent results. The interesting question is about activities characterised by a dip.

Getting past a dip to achieve real mastery is no trivial undertaking. In Malcolm Gladwell's book *Outliers*, he describes the observation that outstanding talent in any field of endeavour requires 10,000 or more hours of effort. Most of us just have the choice between competence and excellence. To achieve excellence, you need to escape the dip.

> to achieve excellence, you need to escape the dip

Success when you are in a dip means working hard – harder than the other people facing the same challenge. Excellence is scarce because few people invest the time it takes to achieve it. So here is why you need to choose: you do not have the time to achieve excellence in everything. To make the time to escape the dip in one area of your life, you must make choices and either give up on other activities, or settle for mere competence.

What you choose to do matters – if you choose a cul-de-sac you will waste your time if you try to get better. If you choose too many skills to develop, you will dissipate your energy and never escape the dips. You have to know when to hold and when to fold.

How to choose

A business case is a document used by commercial, public sector and voluntary organisations to set out the reasons for undertaking a new project or activity. They do this because the resources which they will need to deploy – people, materials, assets and money – are valuable to them, and they want to ensure that they understand the costs, the risks and problems, and ensure that these are more than compensated for by the benefits to come. A business case is like a set of scales, weighing costs against benefits.

Your time is equally precious, so you too should be evaluating the costs and benefits before taking on a new project. The three things to review are the benefits, the cost, and other interesting considerations.

The benefits

Three types of benefit that might justify investing your time:

Goals alignment: how well does this project or activity align with the goals that you have set yourself? Does it come into your Life Will?

Resource generation: what resources will you create from this project or activity that will subsequently help you towards your goals? Activities of this type are enablers of other, goal-driven activities.

Intrinsic value: autotelic activities are the things we do for their own sake – because we enjoy them and get satisfaction from the activity itself.

The costs

There are three areas of cost to consider:

Time cost: inevitably, for the Brilliant time manager, your first consideration is the time you will need to commit, to get it done to the standard you set yourself, or the standard you accept from another person. This is important because if you don't undertake this project you could use the time for something else, so there is what is known as an 'opportunity cost'. This refers to the 'lost' opportunity of not being able to do that other thing.

Resource costs: how much money and other resources (people, materials and assets) will you need to commit, and do you have or can you access those resources?

Risks: what could go wrong? Risks are characterised by an adverse consequence and a probability. The more likely that something is to go wrong, and the harsher the consequence, then the greater the cost that you must associate with the risk.

The interesting things

Three other things to take into account are:

The likelihood of success: how likely are you to succeed? Each of us has a preference for activities with either a high degree of confidence of success or a greater degree of challenge. For all of us, however, there is a confidence level below which we would rather do something else. Do not undertake a project where the chances of success are too remote, or where success depends on a random event that is outside your control.

Consequences of failure: it is also important to understand the consequences of failure. Some of us are great at dusting ourselves down and starting again: others take failure hard and it shakes our confidence. Objectively, what would happen, and subjectively, how would you be likely to cope?

Help and support needed and available: make an inventory of what help and support you would need and then, for each item, examine where it might be available to you. This will give a good sense of how tough a stretching project will be, depending on whether the gap is small or large.

Special time

Here are five types of special time that Brilliant time managers might find helpful. Few will want to use more than a couple of these ideas, but by carving out special time in your week, you will feel that you are more in control and can get more done.

Prime time

We each have times of the day when our energy is high and times when our energy is low. It is at the peaks of your time cycles that you can get most done; this is your 'prime time'. So schedule important tasks into these periods of your day.

People with a lot of discretion over how they use their time often schedule their week into patterns that leave specific slots for different types of activity. For example, they might schedule:

Monday morning, for a reactive response to whatever has cropped up.

Monday afternoon, for quiet thinking and planning time.

Tuesday morning, for appointments and meetings.

Tuesday afternoon, for follow-up actions.

Wednesday morning, quiet time for report and proposal writing.

Wednesday afternoon, for open door – general admin that can be interrupted by informal meetings.

Thursday morning, for appointments and meetings.

Thursday afternoon, for follow-up actions.

Friday morning, for a reactive response to whatever has cropped up.

Friday afternoon, for a review of the week and dealing with contractual, finance and personnel issues.

	Morning	Afternoon
Monday	Reactive response	Quiet thinking and planning
Tuesday	Appointments and meetings	Follow-up actions
Wednesday	Quiet time – reports and proposals	General admin and open door
Thursday	Appointments and meetings	Follow-up actions
Friday	Reactive repsonse	Review and contracts, finance, HR

Golden hour

Photographers refer to the first (dawn) and last (dusk) hour of sunlight during the day as 'golden hour' or, sometimes, as 'magic hour'. The quality of the light creates fabulous photographs. Trauma specialists use the term 'golden hour' to refer to the first minutes to several hours after a traumatic injury, during which prompt medical treatment has the best chance of preventing death, and the victim's chances of survival are greatest. Many writers find there is a golden hour when they can write intensively and produce their best work although, as in the emergency medicine example, it can last even longer. This is the time when authors most easily get into a flow state. A disproportionate amount of this book was written between 6:30 and 8:30am.

If you have a golden hour, then use it. If you suspect you may have one, then try it out. Magic can happen. For night owls, it may be in the peace and quiet when the rest of the household has gone to bed and the streets outside are quiet. For larks, it may be at the very start of the day, before anyone else is up, and when their brains are totally alert.

Creative time

Do you need to be creative in your work? Would you like to be more creative, day-to-day? Creativity thrives on the right conditions, so carve out high-quality time for creativity and set up the right conditions:

Stimulation

Creativity is stimulated by all sorts of different things, whether it is a walk to the shops, a trip to the riverside, browsing through books, or looking at photos. Set up a wealth of opportunities to stimulate your creativity, like trips to museums and galleries, conversations with people in unfamiliar jobs, or participation in unusual activities. If you choose to stay in, fill your working space with all sorts of different stimuli, and change them frequently. Buy a different random magazine each month, put six different postcards on the wall each week, collect found objects wherever you go.

Light and colour

Many of us find bright sunlight is the most stimulating light, but whatever works for you, use it. Different colours have a different effect on our thinking patterns, so choose the prevailing colour in your surroundings to stimulate your creative juices. Here are some typical colour associations:

- Blue: peaceful, harmonious, calming, good for thinking and problem solving.
- Green: relaxing and energising.
- Yellow: energising and positive, good for creativity.
- Pink: loving, friendly, approachable.
- Orange: cheerful, happy, warm.

Energy

Make sure you have plenty of energy, because when we are tired, creativity is one of the first things to suffer. Good rest, good food and good exercise all contribute to building your creative capabilities.

Relaxation and comfort

We are at our most creative when we feel comfortable and can relax – but not so comfortable that there is no drive to create. Creativity also requires a little bit of pressure, either externally imposed, or self-generated.

Company

You will know whether you feel at your most energised when you are in company or when you are alone. Harness this knowledge to create the right social environment for yourself.

The next bend

For some people, the most valuable time in their week is 30 minutes to an hour of high-quality, time-limited thinking time, which they set aside to think about what they don't have time to think about at any other time; the things they are missing when they look at their plans, the questions they haven't yet thought to ask, or the new ideas that will take their thinking, their products or their services forward to the next stage.

So why is it that so few of us carve time out of our working week to do nothing other than think? Could it be that sitting in a quiet place with nothing but a coffee, and maybe a notebook and pen, does not feel like work? If it moves your thinking forward, or anticipates a problem, or resolves a knotty problem, then it is more than just 'work', it is real-value creation.

The best place to look around the next bend is informal and relaxed; a coffee shop, your sofa, a pleasant meeting room, a hotel foyer. Do it on your own, or do it with colleagues, but whatever you do, just do it.

Focus time

If you only had fifteen minutes, what could you do? You might surprise yourself. Focus time is the short periods of otherwise useless time when you can focus hard and get something valuable done ... or just do nothing.

You can use your spare minutes well in lots of different places: an airport lounge, a station platform, or in a waiting room. Two special opportunities are on your daily commute and in the half hour before a meeting that you have travelled to.

Your daily commute

How long do you spend commuting? If you have a half-hour train journey in each direction, then you have five hours a week and, since most of us work around 45 weeks a year, that equates to a massive 225 hours, or the equivalent of over 32 seven-hour days. What project could you tackle if I gave you six whole weeks to do it? I could write a book.

Before your meeting

If you have to travel to a meeting, then you want to be there early to make sure that delays don't cause you to be late. So why not aim to be there half an hour to an hour early, so you can relax at a local café, buy yourself a drink and do something valuable, like prepare for the meeting, review a proposal or report, phone your plumber, write an article, or fill out your expenses form.

Preparedness

The difference between focus time and wasted time is in preparedness: always carry a notebook and pen, your to-do list, a book or magazine to read, the papers you need to work on, and your phone and address book so you can make calls. If you are an office or knowledge worker, a 'mobile office kit' need weigh very little and take up virtually no room. Mine has a pencil and pen, a highlighter, sticky notes, some paper clips, an envelope and a small notepad as well as my notebook. I also carry a memory stick, a small pen-knife, and a phone that does more than the computers NASA used to send men to the moon.

brilliant recap

- Get yourself into a flow state by making even the dullest activities into a challenge that will stretch you to achieve the highest standards.

- Successful people choose which projects to pursue and which to drop. Their ruthlessness about dropping things is what allows them to excel at the things they choose to pursue.

- Evaluate your opportunities by considering their potential value, their costs and how much each one interests you.

- Use the special times in your week to get masses done; times when you work best, when you can be creative, can look ahead, and can focus on something valuable.

CHAPTER 8

Who are you doing things for?

You have learnt about how to be effective in using the time you have, and know how to establish your priorities and avoid time stealers. But do you find yourself spending a lot of your valuable time doing things for other people? You will certainly know the answer to this question if you spent some time keeping a time log, as described in Chapter 2. If you do, you are not alone. Brilliant time managers are able to limit the time they spend doing things for others, to make more time to do things for themselves.

But it is important to be clear that *there is nothing wrong with doing something for someone else.* What is important is your reason for doing it. This will dictate how you feel about that time, and whether you consider it to be time wasted, or time well spent.

A donkey's lot in life is to fetch and carry. They don't have any freedom to choose what they do, so they just get on with it and bear their load stoically. If you are a bit like a donkey, then you probably hide your feelings and don't show the world the toll the stress is taking on you until it is too late, and you feel ground down and resentful.

On the other hand, dogs are eager to make their owners happy, and will do anything that is asked of them just to please other people. If you are a bit like a dog, then you will be a great team player but will rarely give yourself a chance to do what you want, and please yourself.

If you are like a donkey or a dog, then you are probably not doing enough things for yourself and you will come to resent the things you do for other people – and, eventually, resent the other people too. Brilliant time managers also do things for other people, but they do so for their own reasons, when they choose to. For them, helping someone out enhances their lives, rather than diminishes them. They know when to do something for someone else, and when to say 'no'.

This chapter is all about when and how to say 'no'. We will start with the consequences of getting it wrong, and how accumulating other people's jobs is like having a load of monkeys on your back. Then we will focus on how to say 'no', by transforming it into something noble. We will end with saying 'yes'.

Do you have a monkey on your back?

'Mike, I wonder if you could help me with a small problem ...'

'I'd love to,' I reply, 'but I'm very busy right now. I'll tell you what; leave it with me.'

Can you see where I went wrong? Four words there are deadly: 'Leave it with me'. Those four words invite the other person to drop their problem on your shoulders. Now I have a monkey on my back, and it's not even mine. But I still have to look after it and see that it's cared for. Of course that poor monkey is not alone, it is competing for attention with all of the others – my monkeys and other people's monkeys that I have offered to carry around. The monkey metaphor was first suggested by William Oncken Jr, in the early 1970s.

Ten minutes later, I bump into someone else: 'Mike, about that thing you were going to do for me ...'

I have to make a profuse apology; I've been busy. 'Sorry, I'll get right on it and deal with it next.' So now who is controlling my time? Anyone but me, it seems.

Monkeys at work

At the start of your career, you will often thrive by saying 'yes' to any challenge, and then working full tilt to deliver. This will get you a great reputation as a doer. As your career and reputation progress, these calls on your time will increase, and now you need to avoid saying 'yes' quite as often. Monkeys will start to come from further afield, and as you are promoted they will start to come from below: the people that work for you will start to bring you their problems.

As you gather other people's monkeys, you will begin to find it impossible to keep them all fed and watered. And as for your own job … Now that will start to suffer, as you find yourself serving everybody else's monkeys. You may have started off like a dog, all eager to please so that you can progress, but now you are in danger of ending up like a donkey – bent and bowed under the weight of too many of other people's monkeys.

The final stage will see you working late to deal with all your new responsibilities. If you don't deal with the monkey I left with you this morning, then you will find yourself to be the road-block who is stopping me from getting on with my work when I come to you for the answer tomorrow. You may be my boss, but now you are working for me!

Monkeys at home and at play

Monkeys are not just a feature of work life; we have them at home and at play: our children's homework, your neighbour's DIY problem, the cake for the local fête, or walking your mum's dog.

Some monkeys are a pleasure to look after; some are a duty you readily accept. Others, however, are resented intrusions on your life. Accepting these will make you miserable, so the best thing to do is to not accept them.

Managing monkeys

The key to managing monkeys is to spot them coming and to recognise them for what they are – a potential commitment to do something. Once you do this, and declare there to be a monkey, there is a three-step process to managing it: what, who, and how.

What?

The first step is to describe exactly what the monkey is – it is the thing that needs to be done next. Be sure that you and the other person have a shared understanding of what this is.

Who?

Next, allocate the monkey to the most appropriate person. There are three scenarios, depending on the relative power and authority of you and the person who brings the monkey to you.

If you are the senior person, such as the boss in work, a parent, or a sports captain, then you should ensure that you only take the monkey if the other person is truly unable to handle the next step safely. One way to hand back as many monkeys as possible is to specify the simplest next step to take. If your young child wants you to cut up some plastic for a craft project, then clearly you can't leave the knife, and its attached monkey, with them. But you can ask them to gather all of the things they need neatly onto the table. If your subordinate at work wants you to make an important decision, you can ask them to go and think about the options and prepare a recommendation for you, with accompanying evidence.

If you are equals, as you will be in most social situations, or when a peer asks for your help at work, you have the right to say no if their request does not fit with your priorities. The two principal reasons to accept a monkey in this situation are either because doing this will give you pleasure, satisfaction or peace of mind, or because doing it will enhance a relationship with the other person, which you value.

If you are the junior person, you do have a right to say no and seek to reject the monkey, but be aware that they may also have the right to force the monkey on you. So, in rejecting the monkey, you must give them a good reason for re-thinking their strategy. We will examine how to do this in the next section.

The most important thing is that you part with each of you being clear who will care for the monkey. If the monkey is confused, then the poor creature will have one leg on your back and one on the other person's. As you go your separate ways, the monkey will be stretched until, out of self-preservation, it drops to the floor, to be left unloved and uncared for. Now each of you thinks the other is taking care of the monkey, but in truth no one is.

How?

In assigning the monkey to the more junior person – whether you are rejecting someone else's monkey or trying to off-load one of your own – it is vital that you consider what can go wrong. Both the monkey and its carer must remain safe at all times.

If you give me a monkey that I don't have the skills to care for, then not only can the monkey be harmed, but so can I. At the very least, it can knock my confidence, and my performance of other tasks may suffer. So determine how you will ensure that the monkey stays well, by first describing it as a sufficiently small first step, and then agreeing how you will check up on it. Here are seven examples, ranging from a small monkey, passed to an inexperienced person, to a large monkey, given to someone with a depth of relevant skills.

> determine how you will ensure that the monkey stays well

1. 'Here is what I would like you to do now. Let me know as soon as you have done it.'

2. 'What I'd like you to do is think about how you could handle this and come and discuss your ideas with me at 3pm this afternoon.'

3. 'I would be interested to hear your recommendations on how to tackle this, so come and see me when you are ready to share them.'

4. 'Have a go at what you think is the first step; then let's talk about what next.'

5. 'This is your responsibility; let's review how you are getting on at ten o'clock each morning.'

6. 'I would like you to handle this, and perhaps we can get together two or three times to review your progress.'

7. 'This is a challenging problem. I will leave it to you to figure it out, and let me know how it goes.'

N.O.

When we say 'yes' to too much – either for donkey-like reasons of obligation, or dog-like reasons of wanting to please – we lose control of our time. However, the alternative, saying 'no', is hard. We all know it is important to be assertive, but this does not make it easy!

Why 'no' is difficult

Saying no is difficult because it sounds negative. That is why, when we do say no, we often start with *'I am sorry, but ...'* The impact of the 'but' is to tell the listener that the important bit is what comes next, so the only effect that 'I am sorry' has is to make *you* feel bad about saying no.

Why 'no' is good

If you do say yes often, it may make you popular. People will like you for being obliging and they will respect your ability to get things done. But if you say 'yes' to everything, it won't make you any more popular, nor any better respected. Instead, people will see you for what you are: a donkey or a dog – either a beast of burden to be taken advantage of, or a willing puppy who wants everyone to love them.

> if you say 'yes' to everything, it won't make you any more popular

When you learn to say yes or no according to a carefully chosen priority, then you will be more respected and, because you will get done the things you commit to, you will be better liked too. You will transform yourself from a doormat doer to a strategic chooser.

brilliant tip

Say no to perfect. Perfectionism is one of the biggest time thieves of all. Set criteria for 'just right' and as soon as you reach it, stop.

Assertiveness

Assertiveness is all about respect. A passive response in which you say yes to everything shows very little respect for yourself, while an aggressive attitude of saying no to everything anyone else asks you to do suggests you respect yourself above anyone else. Assertiveness is all about respecting other people and yourself equally, and making a choice whether to say yes or no based on the circumstances of each situation.

Passive behaviour

Passive behaviour is characterised by submitting your legitimate needs and desires to those of other people. It makes you afraid to disagree or say no, and if you do, you will feel guilty. It also makes it hard for you to ask for help.

Aggressive behaviour

Aggressive behaviour puts yourself ahead of others and rejects their real needs. You will say no with little thought for the other person, and demand what *you* want rather than ask politely for help when you need it. You will blame other people when things do not go your own way.

Assertive behaviour

Saying no when it is right to do so is assertive behaviour. Here, you will be confident of yourself and of your analysis of the situation. You will ask for the help you need and respect other people's right to say yes or no. To be assertive, you must do what is right; not what is easy. Saying no must feel noble.

From no to N.O.

Assertive behaviour requires us to act nobly, to do what is right. If 'no' sounds negative to you, what could be more positive than nobility? Rather than say no, which sounds negative, make a *Noble Objection*.

A Noble Objection, or N.O., is a no for the right reasons. When you make a N.O., you are declining to say yes, because to do so would be to make a commitment, and conscientious people will always honour their commitments.

Recognise what is important – and to whom – and then make a choice:

- Will you say yes, because it is the right thing to do?
- Will you make a N.O. because saying no is the right thing to do?

How to make a N.O.

When you say no in the form of a Noble Objection, three things will help the other person to feel comfortable with your decision.

The power of empathy

First, you must show them that you understand their situation and why they have asked you. If you don't do this, then they will not accept your N.O. as noble: how can it be well-motivated if you don't understand the situation?

> 'Thank you for asking me to do this. I do understand why it is important to you. I cannot help you with it now.'

The power of options

If you are able to, then suggesting some alternatives will be great help to the other person.

> 'I cannot help you with this. I could recommend that you look at/speak to/start with …'

The power of 'because'

Sometimes it is important for us to understand why someone has made the choice they have made. Explaining your decision is not to 'justify' it, nor to make you feel better; it is to help the other person understand why it was a *Noble* Objection. 'Because' demonstrates the strategic reasoning you have chosen.

> 'I cannot help you with this. I have chosen to prioritise that, which is more important, because …'

Saying 'yes'

Integrity means only making commitments that you will honour. A 'yes' is a whole-hearted commitment, so only say yes when you intend to accept responsibility:

- When the task will move you towards one of your goals or outcomes.
- When the task will give you pleasure, fun or satisfaction.
- When the task is your job, your duty, or your responsibility in the first place, resulting from a former yes. Remember

that, when you sign a contract and accept a job, you are saying a big YES to a whole bunch of tasks.

● When saying yes will enhance a relationship or bring a reward that you value, and the price of committing to the task is proportional to the gain.

Every time you say yes, be sure that it is a conscious choice, that you mean it, and that you want to say yes for one reason or another. Otherwise you will be in danger of becoming either a donkey, or a dog.

 brilliant recap

● When you do things for other people, don't do so simply as a burden, or just to please them.

● Avoid accepting other people's monkeys – their burdens – just because they ask you to. Instead, find ways to manage the situation so that you can help them, while leaving the responsibility with them.

● Spot opportunities to say no to requests for help, work, or contributions that do not contribute to what you must or want to be doing.

● When you do say no, do so for the right reasons – make a Noble Objection.

● When you say yes, do so for the right reasons – make a whole-hearted commitment.

Ultimate success in getting things done

Part 3 of *How to Manage Your Time* will take you beyond the basics of Part 1, and beyond the solutions to the problems described in Part 2, to the techniques that will make you a master of getting things done. You will learn:

- The art of effective delegation and how to overcome your hesitancy to delegate in Chapter 9: Using other people to get things done.

- The ultimate process for how to manage your time in Chapter 10, where you will see how the four-step OATS principle can put you in control of your time.

- The three things exceptional time managers do: planning ahead, working diligently and the OODA Loop, in Chapter 11.

CHAPTER 9

Using other people to get things done

E ventually, no matter how well you are using your time, you will hit a limit to the amount you can get done. Now you need to free up the resources to move to the next level of productivity. You need to not just manage *your* time; you need to start to manage other people's time, too.

If you are doing things that other people could be doing equally well – or better – then you are not getting the most from your time. Delegation is an essential part of your time management repertoire. This chapter will give you all you need to delegate effectively: an understanding of what it is – and is not; ideas about when to delegate – and not; how to get past the mental blocks that stop you from delegating; and, crucially, a five-step process for how to delegate.

What is delegation?

Delegation of work is giving somebody else the responsibility to do something that was originally your own responsibility. At the same time, you must also give them the authority they need to do it and to make any necessary decisions. However, you remain accountable for the work, and so you must retain sufficient control to manage the risks that arise from the situation.

Compare this with the allocation of work. In this case, the work you are giving someone is not yours, but work for which they share responsibility with others. If you have three staff, with a range of responsibilities, you can allocate particular work among them. The people you allocate to are accountable for their work, as well as responsible for it, because it is a part of their job.

When to delegate

There are a lot of good reasons to delegate work. It can:

- Boost the morale of children, team members, or staff, by giving them new challenges
- Demonstrate your trust and the confidence you have in other people
- Build confidence, through tackling new and challenging tasks
- Share your work with others and allow the team to accomplish more
- Increase the responsibility other people take in the overall workload
- Introduce new ideas into established activities
- Develop other people's skills and give them new experience
- Allow you to evaluate someone's learning by offering them a chance to use and test it.

delegation is a good thing

So, delegation is a good thing. It allows you to get more done, develop and motivate people, and create better results for yourself, your family, your club, or your organisation. We can summarise the reasons in two principal areas: first, efficiency and effectiveness – it gives you the time to do the tasks that only you can do, and allows you to have worry-free business trips and holidays; and second, personal development – it helps to enhance skills, creativity, experience and initiative; and it can increase motivation by making people feel valued and worthy of higher-level work.

... and when not to delegate

However, some people delegate for the wrong reasons. Here are some examples of when not to delegate:

- To offload dull work that you really can't face doing.
- To set somebody up to fail by giving them a task they cannot succeed at.
- To avoid responsibility for a task that will almost certainly go wrong.
- When you have been specifically asked to do the work.
- When the other person does not have sufficient ability or confidence to do the task to the standard required.
- When the other person is already overloaded.
- As a punishment – in this case, be open about your intent to reprimand.
- To take advantage of someone's generosity and willingness to help.

It is important to realise that delegating work effectively will not always save you time. Proper handover and supervision takes time, but it is essential to the success of your delegation process.

What stops you?

Despite knowing that delegation is the right thing to do, many of us use it far too rarely. We make all sorts of excuses.

Excuses

What excuses do you use? Do you often use the same one, or do you have a few to choose from? Here are ten common excuses, and why they don't necessarily make sense.

'I'd be better off doing it myself'

In what ways would you be better off delegating it? It may seem easy just doing it yourself, but you won't know unless you try. And even if you are better off, what about the other person? Part of your role may be to help them to learn and develop.

'I don't want to overload my family, my colleagues, my staff'

How many of them really are overloaded? If you plan the team's workload properly, and share your delegation around, you may well be able to delegate without overloading anyone.

'If only I had someone I could delegate to'

Who are you missing when you say that? Make sure you survey all of the people available to you, and understand fully their capabilities and the time they have available.

'I don't want to lose control'

What do you mean by control, and how can you delegate and maintain the control that you want? This is all about putting in place appropriate mechanisms that allow you to feel that the work is in safe hands and that you can check when you need to, to minimise the risks.

'I don't have the time to delegate'

Yes, delegation takes time, but if you have time to do it yourself, then you have the time to delegate. If you get into the habit of delegating and other people learn how to do the tasks well, how much time could you free up over the coming months, and what could you do with that time?

'I'll only end up doing it all again myself'

How often have you thought that and been wrong? This presumes that you have chosen someone who is not capable of doing the work to a high enough standard. But by selecting the right person, briefing them well, and overseeing their work, you can certainly prevent that.

'I want to stay indispensable'
Don't we all? But if you were really indispensable, how could your employer afford to promote you? What is more valuable to most societies, clubs or businesses is not someone who can 'do it', but someone who can build a team of people who can all do it.

'I know exactly how I want it done'
That is fine, but is your way the only way it can be done? Can there be a way that is, maybe, even better? And even if your approach is really the only way, how does that preclude someone else doing it? All that you need to do is ensure you brief them fully on your approach.

'If I ask him/her to do it, he/she will be nagging me every five minutes'
If you want to develop someone, your fundamental job is helping them succeed, so maybe the 'nagging' is part of the territory. However, proper briefing and scheduled progress reviews can reduce this, so develop a plan that balances their need to refer to you, and your need to get on with your work.

'I don't know how to delegate'
Well, hold on then, because once we have examined a few mental blocks, the next section will give you a robust five-step process that will allow you to do just that.

Mental blocks

All of these excuses are often just the superficial reasons we give for not delegating. What lies beneath them are deeper psychological concerns with asking someone else to do something for us: it just doesn't feel right. This triggers guilt, so we avoid the guilt by avoiding trying to delegate.

The psychological theory of Transactional Analysis suggests that we behave in three modes, which it describes as Parent State, Child State and Adult State.

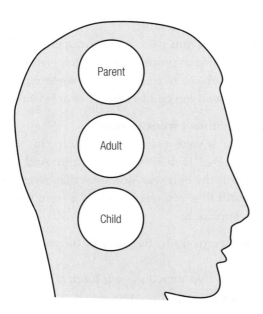

Parent State

The Parent State is where we show our caring aspect; displaying concern for another's welfare, allowing us to explore and trying to help, so that we feel that delegating can be an unfair imposition. Parents also tell you what to do, and expect conformity with tradition. We know this isn't always an appropriate way to deal with people, so we shy away from exhibiting this aspect of ourselves, especially when we sense ourselves becoming judgemental and over-bearing.

Is there a Parent State in you that you feel uncomfortable with? Does asking someone to do something feel too much like 'telling them what to do'?

Child State

Children try to please: to please parents, authority figures and peers. Their primary drive is obedience and a strong need to fit in. If you have been promoted at work, or in a sports club, and still feel that the people you manage – to whom you could delegate – are your equals, or even, perhaps, have more experience than you, then the Child State in you may be anxious and nervous about asking other people to take on work for you.

Is there a Child State in you that is nervous about asking for help from someone who might reject you, belittle you, or make you feel like they are doing you a big favour?

Adult State

In the Adult State, we will assess everything in a calm and rational way. Here, we listen hard, try to understand and apply our knowledge and experience. We are open to assess a situation in the light of evidence and seek to do the right thing, using a sound and fair process. We delegate best when we act from the Adult State and address others in their Adult State.

You are an adult in an adult world. If you have a role that gives you the authority to delegate, then you have a right and, indeed, a responsibility to do so. If you follow a sound process and do so respectfully, then you will find yourself earning the respect you deserve.

How to delegate

Delegation works best when you get every component right. Here is a five-step process to follow.

A five-step process for delegation

Step 1. Matching

Match the task to the person. This has two elements:

Select the task carefully

Make a list of jobs you might delegate. Suitable jobs may be ones that take up a lot of your time, have a lower level of responsibility, or offer a good development opportunity.

Select personnel carefully

Consider who would be suitable. Is there someone who has the time to do it? Is there an individual who needs a challenge? Will the person you select take on the task with enthusiasm? Make sure you choose someone who has the right level of ability to tackle the task, or rise to the challenge, without becoming swamped and demoralised by it. It is also good to choose somebody with the confidence to disagree with you. This way, you may find that they can improve on how you would have done it.

> ensure you are fair
> in the way you offer
> opportunities

Consider too how others might react. Ensure you are fair in the way you offer opportunities, and give everyone a chance to ask questions.

Step 2. Briefing

Meet in an appropriate place and allocate enough time to explain the task fully. The box below sets out what makes a Brilliant briefing. Explain why you have chosen to delegate this job to this person, and set the task in context. Delegation works best when you delegate responsibility for a *whole* task or project, rather than a part of one.

Discuss the level of ongoing support that will meet their needs and your desire for control, so that you can reduce the risk to them and to your organisation to an acceptable level. Ensure that they understand the level and scope of their authority to act, and be ready to confirm this in writing.

 **tip**

A watertight briefing

To create a watertight briefing, remember the acronym: BOAT TAR. The boat is essential, the tar makes it watertight. BOAT TAR stands for:

Background

Explain the context and the history of how the task arose, the 'why', and who are the people involved. Be clear what needs to happen.

Objectives

What will success look like? Be clear about the end result and any interim objectives. Where appropriate, set out the specifications or quality standards you require.

Authority

Be clear about the level of authority you are giving, ranging from: 'consider the task then make your recommendations for my approval', to 'do the task and then let me know how you have done'.

Time

Set a deadline for completion and, if it will help you oversee the process, also establish interim milestones that will track progress and provide momentum and success points along the way.

Tasks

If you are delegating to someone with little experience or expertise, you may choose to lay out some or all of the component tasks, to ensure they know what to do. The more experienced they are, the less guidance you should give. If in doubt, only be prescriptive where there is otherwise an unacceptable risk. We all learn best by making one or two mistakes.

Admin

What administrative arrangements do you want the person you have delegated to to make? Examples include reporting – formal or informal – and notifications of their role to other people.

Resources

Explain what resources are available to support the work. These may include: budget, staff, materials, equipment or accommodation.

Step 3. Commitment

This is where delegation often goes wrong: the person delegating the work fails to get a commitment from the other person, and the work does not then get done or is done in an unsatisfactory manner. All kinds of excuses and recriminations then emerge, that do neither of you any good.

There are three types of commitment that you must obtain, and in exchange you will offer one commitment of your own.

Get a commitment of understanding

Make sure that the person you are delegating to fully understands what you expect of them. Give them an opportunity to ask questions and be patient in answering their concerns.

If you take a shortcut here, you leave yourself open to 'you didn't explain it properly'. Complete the discussion by asking for their confirmation that they understand what you expect of them.

Get a commitment of capability and capacity

When they understand what you are asking them to do, the next thing to confirm is that they feel they have the skills and experience to undertake the work or, if they do not, that you both have a shared understanding of the support that they need. This is a matter of risk management – you must not set them up to fail. It is, however, okay for them to make mistakes. You also need to secure a commitment that they have the time available to give the job the attention that it needs.

If you take a shortcut here, you leave yourself open to 'you asked me to do something I couldn't do'. Complete the discussion by asking for their confirmation that they are able to do what you expect of them.

Get a commitment of willingness

The final confirmation is to get a clear and explicit statement that, as well as understanding what you want and confirming they are able to do it, they are willing to do it and therefore *will do it.*

Offer your commitment to support

You have received a real commitment and, like any contract, you must offer a commitment in return. Having identified the support that the person you have delegated to needs to feel safe and be able to succeed, you must make them an explicit commitment to provide that support. If you know that you are unable to meet that commitment, then do not delegate the work to them.

Step 4. Monitoring

Keep an eye on progress without stifling creativity by ensuring that your level of monitoring is appropriate to the task and the individual. Check progress regularly with brief, well-structured reviews in which you recognise, encourage and praise successes.

Make yourself available if the person you have delegated to gets stuck. Allow them to make mistakes; that is how many people learn, so be supportive. Avoid giving advice if you can; rather, ask questions and encourage them to think through their own solutions. If you interfere by suggesting how you would do the job, by making decisions for them, or suggesting that you may doubt their ability, you will not only undermine confidence but you will also stifle learning.

How you conduct your reviews is something you will have discussed at the Commitment step. They may be informal or on a regular cycle, rather than ad hoc, but you also need to consider how frequently they should be. What setting is right: formal or informal, your space or theirs? Will you ask for written reports in a work context, as well as oral reports, and what documentation will you want to see?

One of your principal roles is to oversee the management of risk. Help the other person think through what can go wrong in the next stage, and what steps they can take to minimise the threat.

Check that they have a fall-back plan in case things do go wrong and ensure they feel confident that you will take a constructive and non-judgemental approach to setbacks and failure. If you fail to do this, then they may well hide bad news from you.

Five things you may want to discuss at each meeting are:

1. General situation.
2. Successes and achievements.
3. Complications, issues and emerging risks.
4. Problems to resolve.
5. Recommendations to review.

Step 5. Feedback

When the job is done, you need to conduct one more review of performance. Allow them to assess themselves: how well did they think they got on?

Recognise their successes and give plenty of praise for their achievements. If they performed particularly well, then a handwritten note has special power to demonstrate your gratitude and will reward them. Also, help them to understand and learn from any problems or failures, and identify what they could do differently next time.

 **brilliant** recap

- Delegating is a key part of time management which gives you more time than you would have on your own.

- Only delegate for noble reasons – don't use it as a way to dump jobs you really ought to do yourself.

- Lots of things can feel like they get in the way of delegating, but none of them needs to. Recognise when you have the right to delegate, and understand that what is going on in your head need not stop you.

- If you want to make sure your delegation works, use a five-step process of matching, briefing, commitment, monitoring and feedback.
- Make your briefing watertight with the seven elements of BOAT TAR.

CHAPTER 10

The OATS principle: the ultimate process for how to manage your time

All of the techniques you have learned so far work really well on their own, or in combination. It is now time to learn a framework that will tie them all together and provide you with a single process that will be the basis for truly effective control of your time.

The OATS principle is an easy-to-follow four-step process for managing your time. It can act as the basis for all of your time management and is consistent with all the techniques you have read about so far. It acts as a single framework – and it is a framework that works.

The origins of the OATS method lie in tried-and-trusted project management principles – it is a simplified version of the way the largest projects are planned, and it is consistent with everything that research into human psychology teaches us.

The OATS principle has four steps, and this chapter examines each step in turn:

Outcomes

Activities

Time

Schedule

When to get your OATS

OATS planning can work on different timescales. You can plan your day, your week, your month, or even your coming year, using this principle. You will find OATS-based planning tools that you can download on the website **www.brillianttimemanagement.com**.

Do you ever find yourself losing sleep because all the things you need to do the next day are running around in your head? If that sounds like you, then you need to get your OATS in the evening, before you go to sleep. On the other hand, if you sleep like a baby, then you can get your OATS in the morning, before you start your day.

Outcomes

OATS planning starts with identifying your outcomes. If you are planning the next day, for example, ask yourself: 'what do I want to be different by the end of the day?' This will give you your outcomes for your day. Similarly, you can also think about your outcomes for the next week, month, quarter or year.

Your outcomes will link to your goals, but they will be narrower in scope. The shorter the period your OATS plan covers, then often the narrower your outcomes will be. Here is an example:

● My goal is to refurbish my home.
● My outcome for this year is to have the lounge and kitchen re-fitted and re-decorated.
● My outcome for the end of the first quarter is to have a design and colours chosen.
● My outcome for April is to appoint tradesmen and agree a schedule with them.
● My outcome for this week is to order all the kitchen units and equipment, the fabrics for the lounge, and the paints.

- My outcome for today is to find a plumber who can come at short notice to deal with the kitchen sink and dishwasher.

A good way to express your outcomes is illustrated in the example above: to state what will be different at the end of the day, or other period.

Outcomes are more flexible than goals

Your outcomes may not all be linked explicitly to your long-term goals. Events have a way of re-shaping your plans without warning and the outcomes you set for tomorrow may be influenced by today's events. For example, if my car breaks down on Monday afternoon, I am likely to add two new outcomes to my OATS plans:

- My new outcome for this week is to have my car fully repaired and roadworthy before the weekend.

- My new outcome for Tuesday is to have an appointment for my car to go into a garage for examination and repair.

More significant work or life events can re-shape your plans for a much longer period.

How many outcomes to set

There are no hard and fast rules about how many outcomes to set. However, since your outcomes will be driving all of your activities, it is helpful if they are memorable. It is also important that each outcome can receive significant focus and attention, or you will run the risk of dissipating your energies too widely. For these reasons, I strongly recommend you set between three and five outcomes per day or per week, and no more than seven.

Over longer time periods, you may feel comfortable setting more outcomes, especially if some of them are narrow and require relatively little work to achieve them. In Chapter 2, we saw that your annual goals might have from two to five big goals and up to seven smaller goals in each area of your life. One or two outcomes for each of these would be appropriate.

 example

Mike's Wednesday OATS plan

First thing on Wednesday morning, I think through what I want to achieve today. I settle on four things:

- By this evening, I will have a completed first draft of Chapter 3 of *How to Manage Your Time*.
- By this evening, I will have a new posting on my blog.
- By this evening, I will have sent off a speaking proposal to Able, Baker and Charlie Ltd.
- By this evening, I will be up to date on my financial admin.

Activities

Once you have determined your outcomes, the next step is to think through the activities you need to carry out in order to achieve each outcome. This process is similar to the popular approach to developing an 'action list' or 'to-do list', but has the advantage that it ensures that each activity on your list is driven by something that you have already decided is important.

The origins of the to-do list

I imagine our ancient ancestors were using to-do lists to make sure that pyramids got built, but the commonest story about their modern origin relates to the early twentieth-century steel magnate, Charles M. Schwab, and a pioneer of public relations, Ivy Lee. The story has it that Lee was working at Schwab's Bethlehem Steel Corporation when he proposed to Schwab that he could make the company more efficient if he could have ten minutes with each of Schwab's top executives.

What he recommended to them all was that at the end of the day each executive sat down and made a list of the six most important things that they needed to get done the next day, arranged in priority order with the most important at the top. When they got to work the next day, they were to address the top one first, then the second, and so on. Any that did not get done would be considered for the next day's list.

So impressed was Schwab with the increased productivity of his senior team, that – according to the story – he paid Ivy Lee $25,000. That was when $25,000 was really a lot of money and, whether the story is wholly true or not, it highlights the value of focusing on getting the most important things done and, therefore, avoiding becoming trapped in the trivia.

The problem with to-do lists

The problem with the way most people use their to-do list is that it combines *everything* that they want to get done, from the trivial to the critical and from the urgent to the aspirational. While this has the merit of gathering everything in one place, it makes it hard to focus on the true priorities.

One way to sort this out is to mark each task with a priority and a great way to do this is to allocate three simple levels of priority:

● Priority A: *'Must do'*
● Priority B: *'Should do'*
● Priority C: *'Could do'*

This approach works well for some people, but it can break down in two ways, so consider these if you try the system out.

Problem number one is that some people have so many items on their 'must-do' list that this process hardly represents a way of prioritising things at all. Problem number two is that we don't tend to do the things we 'should do'. Instead, we waste a whole lot of energy worrying that we should be doing them, without getting on with them. What we do is jump straight from our 'must do' items to the 'could do' items that we want to do because they are more fun. If you are like this and you therefore keep putting your 'should do' tasks back onto your to-do list, day after day, you may be getting quite dispirited by the process, feeling that you aren't making any headway.

The solution to endless 'should do' tasks: your to-don't list

If you spot the same task coming up time and time again on your to-do list, and yet never getting done, there is a simple solution: move it to a new list: your to-don't list. A to-don't list captures all of those things you have kept putting off. Write them out once on your to-don't list and then file that list away. The best place to file it is in the round filing cabinet on the floor by the wall, but if you are not that brave, you can date it and tuck it into a drawer somewhere.

If any of the items on your to-don't list are truly important, they will crop up again. Chances are, however, that these are in no way important, and you have been worrying about them unnecessarily.

Real prioritisation: your today list

My solution to prioritisation focuses on putting the activities that flow from today's outcomes onto a today list. This is not an aspirational long list of things you want to get done: this is a closed list of the things you have decided you will do today. Beneath that list, you can then have a separate list of to-do items. You may also choose to elevate a small number of these one-off tasks to your today list.

Now, you can use your to-do list for what it is best at: recording what you intend to plan into your schedule at a time that suits you, rather than a list of things to do one after the other, as soon as you can.

Today list	
To-do list	

 **example**

Mike's Wednesday OATS plan

First thing on Wednesday morning, I think through what I want to achieve today. I settle on four outcomes. Now, under each of them, I have listed the activities that will contribute to achieving each outcome.

● By this evening, I will have a completed first draft of Chapter 3 of *How to Manage Your Time.*

   – Review my writing plan for Chapter 3.

   – Look up and supplement existing notes on estimation.

   – Devise a way to exemplify the OATS principle.

   – Write Chapter 3.

● By this evening, I will have a new posting on my blog.

   – Flick through my ideas scrapbook for inspiration.

   – Write a blog article.

   – Format and post the blog article.

● By this evening, I will have sent off a speaking proposal to Able, Baker and Charlie Ltd.

▶

- Review yesterday's draft against my meeting notes.
- Print and check for typos and grammar, then make corrections.
- Email proposal to Archie Able and copy it to Charlene Charlie.
● By this evening, I will be up to date on my financial admin.
  - Issue invoice for speaking at Ministry for Time Management annual conference.
  - Check bank accounts for paid invoices.
  - Enter invoices, receipts and payments onto ledger.

Shortening a long to-do list

As you get better at managing your time and getting things done, one of the things you will start to notice is that your to-do list continues to grow, to keep pace with your increasing efficiency. There are three things that you can do to manage this:

● First, you can constantly refer back to your goals and delete items that do not contribute to them.

● Second, any item that hangs around for too long can go onto your to-don't list.

● Third, you can start to cluster groups of tasks into projects and schedule the bulk of the project into the future, setting an appropriate completion date for it. You can then focus on the first item or first few items in the project.

A sense of progress

the longer your today list is, the more you need to feel you are making progress

The longer your today list is, the more you need to feel you are making progress. Your today or to-do list should have space for you to tick off completion. For most people, that tick creates a satisfying sense of completion and marking it allows you to have a little mini celebration – even if all you do is have a stretch or make a cup of tea. There are some people who find that ticking off a completed activity does not have enough physical impact. If you are one of those people, do feel free to draw a line through the item or scrub it out several times. This is one reason why some people don't get on with electronic task managers: there is not enough physical sensation in clicking the completion box.

Where to keep your today and to-do lists

Keep your today or to-do lists handy. Here are eight ways that different people use them – take your pick.

- **Alex** keeps a small pad by his desk on which he makes his list each morning. This allows him to cross through completed items vigorously, and split the page in two to represent his two principal areas of work.

- **Barbara** uses the task list functionality on her email and contact management software. This allows her to categorise tasks, group them, assign priorities and deadlines, and add notes to them. Tools like Microsoft Outlook or Toodledo can work well with the OATS principle.

- **Carlo** relies on the app on his mobile phone. Having downloaded several different ones, he chose one that he likes, and that fits with the OATS principle. What's important to him is having that list with him all the time, and being able to display different aspects of that list.

- **Dinesh** carries a single notebook everywhere he goes. Each notebook he uses is numbered and he keeps notes sequentially, going forward through the notebook, and has a running to-do list at the back. Each day he goes through the list with a highlighter and highlights his today activities.

- **Elena** puts today items onto the relevant boxes of her week-per-view diary and keeps a running to-do list in the

notes section of each week. She then transfers outstanding
to-do items to the next page at the end of the week,
transferring a few items into a to-don't list on a sticky note
in the back of the diary. There is room for two sticky notes,
so when they are both full she throws the older one away
and starts a new one.

● **Funmi** is a bit of a mayfly, so combines all of these
approaches.

● **Gordon** puts sticky notes all over his desk area.
Occasionally one falls off and gets lost. Luckily he has a
laid-back sloth attitude and doesn't care.

● **Hetal** uses a pad of photocopied OATS today templates that
she downloaded from **www.brilliant-timemanagement.com**.

Time

The third step in the OATS process is to consider each activity
you have on your plan for the day, week, month or longer, and
to estimate how much time it will take you to complete them.
This is, perhaps, the trickiest step: most of us are not great at
estimating how long things will take us. So the sections below
will give you advice on how to estimate, and how to get really
good at estimating.

How to estimate

Estimating time is difficult for four main reasons: unrealistic
expectations, unforeseen problems, uncooperative collabora-
tors, and unwanted interruptions. Be aware of these factors
and build them into your estimate and, where you are estimating a sizeable and important activity, you may want to
use several independent techniques and sources to make
more than one estimate. Here are five steps to making a good
estimate.

1. The first thing to ask yourself is 'have I done anything like this before?' If you have, what did you learn? Did you over- or underestimate how long it would take, and how long did it take?

2. Next, are there any rules of thumb that can you can apply? For example, you may have a fair confidence that you can write around 1,000 words of text an hour, so a 4,000-word report would take you around four hours to write. Then ask, how does this situation differ from the typical situation? Maybe you are writing on a very familiar topic, so you could perhaps do 1,500 words per hour. On the other hand, you may need to do some careful thinking and refer to reference sources from time to time; maybe 500 words an hour would be a better estimate?

3. Allow time to review, test and put right your work. If you are doing something where there is any possibility of error (not by you, of course, but by someone less able), then it is safest to assume that what could go wrong will go wrong: your report will have typos and incorrect graphs, you will cut a piece of wood wrong when building your shelves, or you will temporarily mislay an important part for the thing you are repairing.

4. Now think about contingency. Our four difficulties in estimating all point in the same direction, and people consistently underestimate how long individual activities will take. If you have a consistent pattern, you will know how much time to add. If not, then a range of 10–30 per cent contingency can be appropriate, or maybe even higher for unfamiliar or complex work.

5. If you are working as part of a team, then it is as well to be aware that team estimates of the time needed are usually even less reliable – teams massively underestimate the time that tasks will take them. There are two main reasons for this: first, they fail to allow sufficiently for the time

it takes just to manage themselves and negotiate among themselves, and second, there is a sense that everyone wants to appear confident, so that the team eggs itself on to more and more bullish time estimates. For teams, a range of 30–50 per cent contingency can be appropriate, or maybe even higher for unfamiliar or complex work, or new teams that have not worked together.

How to get really good at estimating

The five steps above will give you the best chance of making a reliable estimate. If you want to get really good at estimating, however, then there is a way to hone your skills which has only two steps.

Step one: Make time estimates for *everything* you do. Before you start anything, take a moment to estimate how long it will take you; whether it is making a cup of coffee, walking your children to school, driving a couple of hundred miles, writing a report, mowing the lawn, hanging out the washing … Do you get the picture? Anything. When you make your estimate, aim for as precise a figure as you can, so if you are estimating something that you think will take under an hour, estimate the time to the minute. For something that will take a few hours, estimate it to the nearest five minutes.

_____

make time estimates for *everything* you do

_____

Step two: When you have completed the task, look and see how long it actually took and mentally compare it to your estimate.

There is no third step. Do not try to figure out why your estimate was too big, too small or spot on. With no disrespect, unless something obvious happened, like an accident on the motorway, or you ran out of coffee, you probably won't be able to figure out a pattern to your estimating.

However, there is some really good news. One of the things the human brain is really good at is making patterns. It is so good at this that we do it unconsciously all the time. We even make patterns where none exist, which is why cultures all over the world see patterns in the stars, and children all over the world see shapes in the clouds during day time and in the shadows at night.

So if you practise steps one and two relentlessly, gradually your Brilliant brain will form patterns and will start to work out how to make better estimates, and you will just get better at it. This may take months, or even years, but if you continue practising you will start to notice that your estimates are often uncannily accurate.

Does this mean you will never get it wrong? Absolutely not – it will always be wise to add a contingency because sometimes there will be genuinely unforeseeable circumstances. But it does mean that you will often find things get done faster than you expected, because you still have your contingency time in hand.

> it will always be wise to add a contingency

So, now I have this section written just a little quicker than I planned, I can pop off for a swift cup of tea, before continuing with ...

brilliant example

Mike's Wednesday OATS plan

First thing on Wednesday morning, I think through what I want to achieve today. I settle on four outcomes and, under each of them, I list the activities that will contribute to achieving each outcome. Then I estimate the time that each activity will take me.

▶

● By this evening, I will have a completed first draft of Chapter 3 of *How to Manage Your Time*.

- Review my writing plan for Chapter 3 – 20 minutes.

- Look up and supplement existing notes on estimation – 20 minutes.

- Devise a way to exemplify the OATS principle – 20 minutes.

- Write Chapter 3 – 4 hours.

● By this evening, I will have a new posting on my blog.

- Flick through my ideas scrapbook for inspiration – 15 minutes.

- Write a blog article – 1 hour.

- Format and post the blog article – 15 minutes.

● By this evening, I will have sent off a speaking proposal to Able, Baker and Charlie Ltd.

- Review yesterday's draft against my meeting notes – 20 minutes.

- Print and check for typos and grammar, then make corrections – 20 minutes.

- Email proposal to Archie Able and copy it to Charlene Charlie – 20 minutes.

● By this evening, I will be up to date on my financial admin.

- Issue invoice for speaking at Ministry for Time Management annual conference – 20 minutes.

- Check bank accounts for paid invoices – 20 minutes.

- Enter invoices, receipts and payments onto ledger – 20 minutes.

Schedule

Once you have estimated the time each activity will take, the final step is to schedule each activity into your day. Before you do this, check that your diary or agenda planner is up to date with your fixed commitments, because you will need to schedule your tasks around these. Fixed commitments include things like meetings, duty times, and timetabled activities such as collecting children from school.

C. Northcote Parkinson

Cyril Northcote Parkinson was a junior officer in the British Army during the Second World War. On one day that was to influence his later writings and so give him a measure of fame, the three more senior officers in his unit all had to be away from the base, leaving him as the most senior officer there. Preparing himself to be in charge and to have to do the work of four officers, he got up early and went to his office to await the onslaught of work. And he waited; no onslaught came. He gradually realised that, with his colleagues away, there was relatively little to do, because most of their work was generated by the four of them making work for each other. This was the first of many observations that led Parkinson to formulate Parkinson's Law, that 'work expands to fill the time available for its completion'.

We see Parkinson's Law at work in our own lives. If you have little on, or have little enthusiasm for this morning's main task, dealing with your email or making a shopping list can take up a large part of the morning. If, on the other hand, you have a pressing deadline and so start your day with a big, important activity, finishing it half an hour before meeting somebody for lunch, then you will probably be able to deal with just the same amount of email in that half hour. You've probably noticed the same thing with household chores and in many other contexts.

> we see Parkinson's Law at work in our own lives

Rocks, stones and sand

Stephen Covey popularised a useful illustration. If I put half a dozen rocks into a bucket, until it will hold no more, the bucket looks full. But in fact I can add a large number of stones which will fill the gaps neatly. And this now looks full; I could equally pour in a fair quantity of sand and expect it to fill up the smaller spaces between the stones. Instead, reverse the sequence. Empty the bucket and sort and sieve the rocks, stones and sand into three piles and then put the sand into the bucket first to create a layer at the bottom. Then add the stones to make another layer. When you come to add the rocks, you will now find that they do not all fit.

Time works in the same way. If you start by filling your day with the little bits of sand, you will find there are rocks left over at the end. So the art of scheduling is to start by scheduling the rocks into your day, then fill the gaps with your stones and, finally, fit in the sand around the more important tasks.

Time cycles

The next question is, obviously, 'how do I schedule the rocks?' Here the rule is, subject to any fixed commitments, schedule the big, complex, important activities into time slots where you are at your best. We all have times of the day when we feel great, and other times when we feel sluggish. If you are not a morning person and get to work feeling in desperate need of a hot coffee while you gently become more alert, then starting an important piece of work straight away would be a mistake. Yet if you are at your brightest early in the day, then that's the time to schedule your most important piece of work that demands your utmost focus and concentration.

Plot your time cycle

The diagram opposite illustrates a typical time cycle, with clear places where its owner would focus on their best work, and dips where they would catch up on the small activities that require little concentration. If you want to plot your time cycle, you can download a chart from **www.brilliant-timemanagement.com**. If you have used a time log, as described in Chapter 2, you will have a record from which to do this; otherwise, use what you know about yourself.

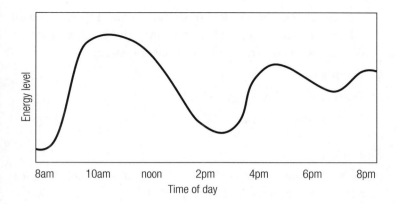

So, are you an early bird or a night owl? Some people really do exhibit a clear pattern, but most of us fall somewhere in between these stereotypes. But what does seem to be true is that our personal pattern is a physiological constraint that we cannot escape. So your best strategy is to work with it.

Modifying your time cycle
Although you cannot change your personal time cycle, you can overwrite it temporarily. Here is a list of things that can boost your energy:

- Sugar (short-term hit).
- Slow-release carbohydrates, such as brown rice (will boost your energy over hours).
- Caffeine.
- Alcohol (small amounts enhance your mood – up or down. Large amounts drain your energy. Note that in many workplaces alcohol is absolutely forbidden, and it will always impair your judgement).
- Water (as your brain dehydrates, it gets less efficient and your thinking slows down, long before you notice tiredness or a headache).

- Chocolate (combines three powerful chemical types: cocoa, a legally available euphoriant; fats, that give a sense of well-being; and sugar, which gives a boost of energy).
- Fresh air.
- Getting up and moving around.
- Deep breaths.

Deadlines

Parkinson's Law can work in reverse. The Stock-Sanford Corollary to Parkinson's Law says that 'if you wait until the last minute, it only takes a minute to do'. This seems a familiar situation to many of us and a lot of people do work that way. In Chapter 5, we saw how it is the favoured style of work for some people with what we described as Octopus personalities.

It is not a method for time management, but it does contain within it a technique. When you set deadlines for yourself or for others, you create a powerful motivating force. When an activity or outcome has no deadline, there can be no failure: it has simply not been achieved *yet*. However, as soon as you introduce a deadline, you can motivate not only the people who find success a powerful driver, but also those who are motivated to avoid failure.

This is particularly true when you accompany a deadline with a commitment. When we commit to a deadline, the little voice in our head, like Jiminy Cricket in *Pinocchio*, will worry away at us as the deadline gets near. Our conscience does not like the conflict between a promise made and the prospect of breaking it – even when we made that promise to ourselves.

to help you get things done, set a deadline and make yourself a commitment

So, to help you get things done, set a deadline and make yourself a commitment. This is why the OATS principle is so powerful; it creates the deadlines and, by writing them down in the form 'by such a time, I will have ...', it helps you to make yourself a written commitment.

 **example**

Mike's Wednesday OATS plan

First thing on Wednesday morning, I think through what I want to achieve today. I settle on four outcomes and, under each of them, I have listed the activities that will contribute to achieving each outcome. Now I estimate the time that each activity will take me and when is the best time of day to do it.

- By this evening, I will have a completed first draft of Chapter 3 of *How to Manage Your Time*.
  - Review my writing plan for Chapter 3 – 20 minutes; 8–9am.
  - Look up and supplement existing notes on estimation – 20 minutes; 8–9am.
  - Devise a way to exemplify the OATS principle – 20 minutes; 8–9am.
  - Write Chapter 3 – 4 hours; 9–1pm.
- By this evening, I will have a new posting on my blog.
  - Flick through my ideas scrapbook for inspiration – 15 minutes; 4–5:30pm.
  - Write a blog article – 1 hour; 4–5:30pm.
  - Format and post the blog article – 15 minutes; 4–5:30pm.
- By this evening, I will have sent off a speaking proposal to Able, Baker and Charlie Ltd.
  - Review yesterday's draft against my meeting notes – 20 minutes; 2–3pm.
  - Print and check for typos and grammar, then make corrections – 20 minutes; 2–3pm.

▶

- Email proposal to Archie Able and copy it to Charlene Charlie – 20 minutes; 2–3pm.

● By this evening, I will be up to date on my financial admin.

- Issue invoice for speaking at Ministry for Time Management annual conference – 20 minutes; 3–4pm.
- Check bank accounts for paid invoices – 20 minutes; 3–4pm.
- Enter invoices, receipts and payments onto ledger – 20 minutes; 3–4pm.

 brilliant recap

● The OATS principle is the ultimate process for how to manage your time.

● First, set out your **outcomes**; what you want to be different by the end of the next day, week, month or year, in the form: 'by ... I will have ...'

● Then list the **activities** that you need to carry out to achieve those outcomes. Place those you need to address in the coming day onto a today list, and others onto a to-do list.

● Estimate the **time** needed for each activity on your to-do list.

● **Schedule** your activities to put the biggest, most complex, and most important activities into the times of the day when you are at your best.

CHAPTER 11

The three things exceptional time managers do

Throughout *How to Manage Your Time,* we have used animals to illustrate the different ways we view or use our time. In this final chapter, we will consider three animals capable of brilliant feats of time management: squirrels, beavers and, at last, people. These are the habits that exceptional time managers cultivate. They go beyond the fundamentals of Part 1 and the remedial techniques of Part 2. They will even take you beyond the power of the OATS process. If you want to be a master of getting things done, you need to learn from:

● Squirrels – and how they plan ahead.

● Beavers – and how they work diligently to change their world.

● The OODA Loop – John Boyd's formula for ultimate success.

Squirrels plan ahead. For them, there is never 'too much opportunity' – in times of plenty, they work hard to store away any surplus as a way to prepare for the coming times of scarcity. They can plan and mitigate the threat of winter ahead. So we will start by looking at those two skills. In English, we talk of 'squirrelling away' stocks and stores.

Beavers work hard to change their environment and build something of lasting value for themselves and their family. So, in the second section, we will focus on working diligently. In English, we talk of 'beavering away' at something.

Finally, there is perhaps no animal metaphor for one aspect of human behaviour: the ability to reflect. Some animals learn from mistakes and others are capable of persevering in the face of setback after setback. But perhaps we are alone in combining analysis, learning, perseverance and reflection. And this is the secret to our success, constantly building on what we have already. For the Brilliant Time Manager, there is no better model to close this book with than the ultimate secret of success, the OODA Loop.

Planning ahead: squirrel time

Planning ahead can mean anything from scheduling a single task into the future to deciding how to coordinate and schedule a whole array of interrelated activities, which we can call 'a project'. If you want to plan ahead, there are three essential things to consider:

1. What do you want?

   Think about your goals and how you will know if you have been successful. We have covered this in Chapter 4.

2. How will you get it?

   This is where you consider the process you will use to achieve your goals and create your plans.

3. What can go wrong?

   It is essential that you give some thought to the problems – or risks – that you may face, and what you are going to do to mitigate them.

Creating plans

The three things that will feature in your plans are timing, tasks and resources.

● Timing gives you an indication of when you want to achieve things by, and therefore when you are going to do things.

● Tasks are the things, or activities, you need to do to achieve your goal.

● Resources are the people, materials, equipment, assets and money which you need to get the job done.

Let's consider these one at a time.

Timing

A great way to plan any project is to start with a set of milestones. A milestone is a point in time when something has happened – usually something significant. So start by thinking through a list of all the significant achievements that you need to gain on the road to completing your project.

Some people like to start with where they are now and work through the project in sequence, right to the end. Others prefer to start at the end with the last milestone – completion. They then work back to the beginning, thinking through what needs to be done before the next milestone. A third group of people have brains like scrambled eggs and they think up their milestones in a random sequence and then sort them into a logical order.

Any approach works. Try writing your milestones onto sticky notes and then arranging them in sequence on a board, a wall, or a large window. When you are happy with your sequence of events, allocate a date or time to each. This gives you a plan for your project.

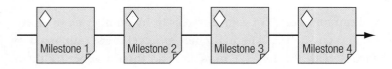

Tasks

You also need to think about all the individual activities that make up your project. The easiest way to do this is to start by splitting your project into chunks, which we will call Level 1. You can do this in a number of ways. For example, you can divide it up by:

- Phases, such as early phase, mid-phase and late phase.

- Zones, such as indoors and outdoors; or Northern office, Midlands office and Southern office.

- Types of work, such as carpentry, plumbing, electrical and decoration; or finance, personnel, IT and facilities.

When you have done this, take each of your chunks (Level 1) and list all of the big things you need to get done. This is Level 2. In a third step, for each of those big things, list all of the individual tasks you need to do. These are Level 3.

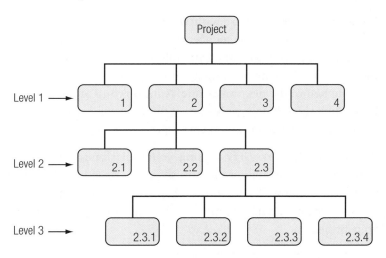

You can number all of your tasks easily, by numbering the Level 1 chunks 1, 2, 3 … The big things at Level 2 are numbered by starting with the Level 1 number, and then numbering them, for example, 2.1, 2.2, 2.3 … Now number your Level 3 tasks, starting with the Level 2 number, such as 2.3.1, 2.3.2, 2.3.3 …

When you break down your work in this way, you are creating what is known as a 'work breakdown structure'.

Resources

The easiest way to determine the resources you need, and to allocate them, is to start with your work breakdown structure. For each task at Level 3, estimate the resources you will need: how much budget, what materials, what equipment or assets, who to help you?

When you focus on the budget, you can add up your estimates at Level 3, to get summaries at Level 2, and then at Level 1. When you add up the Level 1 estimates, you get an estimate of your total budget. You have just created a cost breakdown structure.

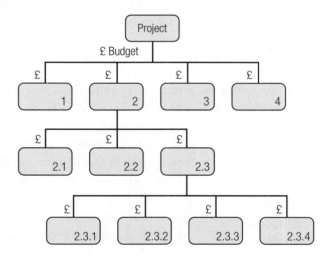

Mitigating risks

Mitigating your risks means either reducing the threat they pose or, if you cannot do this satisfactorily, having a 'Plan B'. Make a list of everything you can think of that could go wrong, and then, for each, rate it as either:

● Red for Danger: there is a good chance of these risks causing significant problems of one sort or another.

    In this case, you need to reduce the threat, and have a Plan B as well.

● Amber for Caution: a significant problem could occur, but it seems unlikely. The only likely problems will be minor.

In this case, you need to either reduce the threat to green, or have a Plan B in case.

● Green for Go: a minor problem that is unlikely to occur.

In this case, you don't need to do anything in advance.

Reduce the threat

How do you reduce the threat of something going wrong? There are two ways. First, you can either find ways to stop it from happening or, if that is not possible, at least make it less likely to go wrong. Second, you can find ways to cushion the blow and make it less serious if it did happen.

Plan B

Having surplus resources, setting aside extra time, and finding alternative solutions are all elements of your Plan B, or contingency plan, that you can invoke when things start to go wrong. However, the ultimate Plan B must also leave you clear as to what you will do if none of these succeed. Having such a contingency plan will give you ultimate confidence that you are in control: you cannot stop things going wrong, but you will know what to do if the universe does decide to bite back.

> having a contingency plan will give you ultimate confidence that you are in control

Working diligently: beavering away

Hard work requires effort, and beavers are certainly not averse to that: they work hard to dam a part of their river or stream so that they can have a still water pool in which to build their lodge. Working hard implies an almost thoughtless focus on the job at hand. It is far better to find a smart way to do the work with minimum effort. You may not be able to find a better way but, whether you can or you cannot, what is often necessary is diligence: a steady and careful application of effort until the job is done.

Diligence and discipline

Diligence requires the discipline to get on with the job at hand, even if it is not what you want to do but is something that you know you must do. For longer jobs, set yourself regular work periods, with targets for each. Remove all sources of distraction, such as email if you are working on a computer. Challenge yourself to not just *do* the work, but to do it *really well*. This can turn a mundane job into a flow task, as we saw in Chapter 7.

You will often find that you can get more done if you set yourself short periods of intense work, and follow them with short breaks. For many people, 25 minutes of work and a five-minute break work well. In the break, you can recharge and refresh yourself, making the next 25 minutes far more productive than the 35 minutes you would have had if you had chosen to work through for a full hour.

> you can get more done if you set yourself short periods of intense work

If you are going to subject yourself to discipline, then it is only fair that you equally reward yourself with decent breaks where you can relax and enjoy yourself. This is also important. Without the chance to rest properly, your capacity for diligent work will start to diminish.

Sustaining momentum

As your projects get longer, the next challenge is to sustain momentum over what can sometimes be a considerable period of time. A three-part process will help you:

1. **Chunk it down**

   Break your project into phases and each phase into manageable chunks, with milestones marking the ends of each chunk and phase.

2. **Schedule the chunks**

   Set aside a definite time slot for each chunk. Make sure that the time available is well-matched to the time needed for the task. Keep up momentum by scheduling a part of the work each day – even if, on a busy day, you only plan to do a very small chunk, like making a phone call, sending an email, sandpapering a piece of wood, stitching a hem or pruning a rose bush.

3. **Celebrate milestones**

   As you complete each chunk, celebrate the completion by noting your success, taking a break and rewarding yourself with a small treat. With bigger milestones, allow yourself bigger celebrations. Plan to mark the end of a project well.

Rust never sleeps

When you have a long-running project, it can be tempting to get caught up in the core activity and miss both the big picture and also the subsidiary details. However, as Neil Young told us in 1979, rust never sleeps, so keep polishing the metal. Here are seven things to focus on, to ensure that you are looking after the basics.

1. **Today list**

   Keep on top of the activities you need to do today.

2. **Quality**

   Review the quality of everything you do.

3. **Milestones**

   Know what milestones are coming up and celebrate those that have been met.

4. **Fizzing bombs**

   Deal with burning issues as soon as possible, before they explode in your face.

5. **Relationships**

   Look after the relationships that matter, or they too will become fizzing bombs.

6. **The next bend**

   Set aside good-quality thinking time, so that you can peer around the next bend and see what's coming before it's too late.

7. **Admin**

   Keep on top of your admin, or it will jump on top of you when you can most do without it. This means filing things so you can find them and returning important documents before you get chased.

Ultimate success: the OODA Loop

Colonel John Boyd was a US Air Force fighter pilot during the Korean War. His colleagues gave him the nickname 'Forty-second Boyd' because of his ability to get behind an enemy plane quickly, and so win aerial dog-fights.

After the war, he became a widely respected military theorist, whose ideas still influence military thinkers around the world. Perhaps his best-known contribution is the OODA Loop. Originally, this was a way of describing military tactics and strategy, based on how he fought aerial dog-fights. His principal argument was that when you go around your OODA Loop faster than your adversary, you would get inside their decision cycle. This puts you in control and the encounter feels to you like it is happening in slow motion.

The OODA Loop is a four-step cycle for success in a changing environment. As you speed up the rate at which you go around the loop, you increasingly gain control of your situation. The four steps are:

Observation

Use all of your senses and resources to gather information from the outside world and identify what is going on.

Orientation

Figure out what your information is telling you, using a combination of analysis and intuitive responses.

Decision

Make a plan and decide what you are going to do, in response to the situation.

Action

Take decisive action.

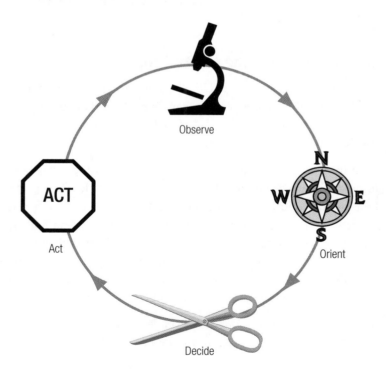

Then observe the outcome of your action, review what you have learned, form a new plan and take further action. If you move fast enough through this cycle, you will be in control of your situation.

The OODA Loop and time management

If you want to use your time to maximum advantage, moment by moment, a fixed plan will let you down. Instead, constantly re-prioritise based on your actual progress, new events and information, and emerging priorities. This is a far better approach than a static schedule, especially in a fast-moving environment.

A far earlier military strategist, Helmuth von Moltke, said: 'No plan of operations extends with certainty beyond the first encounter with the enemy's main strength', often simplified to 'no plan survives contact with the enemy'. As soon as you start to implement your plan it will be out of date. So monitor what's going on, assess how it relates to your resources and objectives, decide what you are going to do next, then act decisively.

 **brilliant** recap

- Plan ahead by thinking about tasks, timing, resources and risks.
- If it is important, then make sure you have a Plan B.
- Keep up momentum by dividing your project into chunks, which you can schedule, complete and celebrate.
- Rust never sleeps – so look after the basics to ensure that nothing important gets missed.
- Remain flexible and be prepared to revise your plans as things change: use the power of the OODA Loop – Observe what's happening, Orient yourself to what it means, Decide what to do next, and take decisive Action.

Conclusion

Getting things done, meeting deadlines, balancing the different areas of your life, and having some day left over at the end of your task list are as much a state of mind as a skill. They require discipline and persistence.

But neither of these can ever be enough on their own. *How to Manage Your Time* offers you the widest possible range of tools and techniques with which you can understand and manage your time. Like any toolbox, the more tools it contains, the more likely it is that there will be just the right tool for the job – whatever crops up.

Each of you is different. You have a different personality, different goals in life, different demands on your time. So each of you will find that different tools help you. I doubt there will be many people who read this book and say 'every single idea will help me', but by the same token I am certain that everybody who reads this book will say 'wow, there are a lot of great ideas, and I know that some of them will really help me.'

If they do, I look forward to hearing from you at **www.brillianttimemanagement.com**.

Further reading

Here are five of the best of the many books about time management:

Focus: Use the Power of Targeted Thinking to Get More Done, Jurgen Wolff (Prentice Hall Business, 2010)

Give Me Time, The Mind Gym (Chartered Institute of Personnel and Development, 2006)

Do it Tomorrow and Other Secrets of Time Management, Mark Forster (Hodder & Stoughton, 2006)

Eat That Frog!: Get More of the Important Things Done, Today!, Brian Tracy (Mobius, 2004)

Time Tactics of Very Successful People, B. Eugene Griessman (McGraw-Hill Professional, 1995)

Here are other books, which cover particular topics in the text:

The Time Paradox, Philip Zimbardo and John Boyd (Rider & Co, 2010)

The Management Models Pocketbook, Mike Clayton (Management Pocketbooks, 2009)

Flow: The Psychology of Optimal Experience, Mihaly Csikszentmihalyi (Harper Perennial, 2008)

The Dip: The Extraordinary Benefits of Knowing When to Quit (and When to Stick), Seth Godin (Piatkus, 2007)

The One Minute Manager Meets the Monkey, Kenneth Blanchard with William Oncken Jr & Hal Burrows (HarperCollins Entertainment, 2004)

Index